MUSIC TO
MY YEARS

A scrapbook of personal
recollections and musings.

John Elm

2QT (Publishing) Ltd

First Edition published 2021 by
2QT Limited (Publishing)
Settle, N. Yorkshire

Cover images: John Elm

Printed by IngramSpark

A CIP catalogue record for this book is available
from the British Library

ISBN 978-1-914083-16-7

DEDICATED WITH LOVE TO

Family and friends who've seen me through life's trials.

ALSO

The Friarage Hospital, Northallerton
St. James's Hospital, Leeds
James Cook Hospital, Middlesbrough
and
every single employee of our wonderful NHS

Contents

Prologue   1

01 The Chauffeur, The Baker, The Secret Codebreaker   4

02 Boomersville   12

03 The Violin Years   22

04 Fifteen Quid Legends   29

05 High Days and Holidays   33

06 Lessons to Learn   39

07 The Lion Awakes   43

08 1966 : The Good, The Bad And The Ugly   49

09 The Chosen Ones and The Beautiful People   55

10 Technological Revolution # 1 – Man On The Moon   61

11 'What You Need Is A Good Bad Woman'   65

12 Halcyon Days   69

13 Fish, Chips and Garlic Bread   76

14 Student Life   79

15 Love amongst the Roundabouts   92

16 Britain at War   101

17 Moving with the Times   103

18 If Music Be The Food Of Love, Play On...   106

19 Learning my Trade   110

20 Mamas and Papas   115

21 The Thatcher Legacy   120

22 Faith, Hope and Calamity   130

23 A Big Mistake   134

24 The Chelsea Flower Show   139

25 Diana   152

26 A Labour of Love   154

27 Technological Revolution #2 — Millennium Bug   159

28 9/11 - Trying to Comprehend the Incomprehensible   164

29 A Few Minutes of Fame   171

30 A Few More Minutes of Fame   177

31 Floods   185

32 From Here to Austerity   187

33 Swansong   191

34 Treasures, Tributes and Obits   197

35 Messing with the Mothership   200

36 Annus Horribilis   211

37 Memo from a Hospital Bed   216

38 Carry on Regardless   222

Epilogue   226

PROLOGUE

THE diagnosis a few weeks previously was unequivocal: I had cancer.

We are constantly reminded of the fact that all of us will, at some time in our lives, have a friend or member of our family afflicted by the disease, so there is no point whatsoever in asking the question why me? Why *not* me? That said, it goes no way to mitigate the initial shock and you'd be inhuman not to have moments of deep despair.

Sitting alone in a hospital room awaiting an operation, I reflected on my circumstances. It's a situation that has confronted thousands before and one which many, to their great credit, have turned into positive action, often attaining levels of achievement they had previously not thought possible. With that in mind, my thoughts returned to a project I had started some years earlier at the time of my sixtieth birthday. I wanted to write something about my life and, more especially, the extraordinary times in which it has been lived.

Previously when putting pen to paper, I was defeated by a lack of incentive and, as someone to whom the written word has never come easily, the sheer enormity of the task. Now this sudden awareness of mortality and uncertainty was tearing away any inhibitions that may have thwarted my ambition. Suddenly my past, which at one time seemed banal, became very precious to me. I was looking at life from a fresh perspective, and I was aware that my destiny was overshadowed by circumstances beyond my control. In short, I had a personal goal to achieve in a time scale that might, or might not, allow me to achieve it.

Looking back over the years, I confess I've not exactly been a hell raiser. I've often been rather intimidated by life itself. Someone having *'no very stable foothold for himself among life's troubles'* is how Robert Louis Stevenson saw his father Thomas, one of the great Scottish lighthouse builders, and it is a description that equates well with how I have blundered my way through life (not that I would presume to draw any other parallels with such genius).

Likewise, my career in the almost totally unrecognised profession of landscape architecture has been rather more cord trousers and muesli than glitz. I have had to accept that I'm not exactly one of life's movers and shakers, but I'd like to think my passage might be something with which you, as you read this, may feel some empathy. At least you can take succour from knowing you're not the only one to screw-up.

I know for a fact that I'll not be able to help you with *life, the meaning and all that*, but I've seen and experienced enough to believe that life is a gift, though living can be a trial that leads many, including myself, to question that belief.

But if life hasn't quite delivered as I would have liked it to, I've been fortunate enough to live during a seminal period in history, a time of freedom, optimism, social enlightenment, technological advancement and great creativity within the arts. Sadly, it seems these phenomena have not worked to the long-term betterment of society. During the last thirty years or so, we seem to have grown ever more divided, decadent and violent, and are presided over by inept politicians who frequently place self-interest before the wellbeing of the nation via a political system that is both outdated and undemocratic. Not only that, we face new worldwide challenges that may outstrip our ability to solve them despite all the technological progress that we've achieved.

It is my intention to revisit in your company many of the defining moments in our recent history, good and bad, and other events that have informed my life and the wonderful yet often troubled world in which we all reside. To help me with my memoir, I've illuminated the text with references to the many songs and songwriters whose contributions to, and observations on, this remarkable period are very precious to me.

I will, of course, refer to my family background and personal experiences, but I believe the building blocks that form a person's character are rather more complex than the immediacy of one's upbringing, important though it is. What I really want to do is to navigate the course of my life through the context of world events and to assess how they, along with my personal circumstances, have influenced my thoughts and made me the person I am today.

If I can also ruffle some feathers and raise a few establishment eyebrows without becoming the ubiquitous Grumpy Old Man, then my job here will be well done.

No matter how you look at it, life is complicated. It is informed by other people whom we meet and sometimes love, and whom we lose to time or circumstances. The simple fact that you are reading this, means our paths are crossing to some extent. To that end, I'd like to think that, at this very precious moment, you are sipping Prosecco and reading from some well-thumbed and dog-eared copy of this book that has found its way into your Tuscan holiday villa. Or maybe you're sitting in a B&B in Ambleside, flipping the pages whilst watching wisps of low cloud kiss the Langdale Pikes. Better still, you've just found me, all crisp and new, wedged tightly between Katherine Jenkins and Geri Halliwell in the biography section of your local branch of Waterstones, WH Smiths or a similar establishment.

Now there's a thought I wish I'd had while I was sitting in the pre-op room. It would have been a nice fantasy to take with me as I awaited the attentions of the anaesthetist.

01

THE CHAUFFEUR, THE BAKER, THE SECRET CODEBREAKER

HAVE you ever looked in the bathroom mirror and thought, 'Who the hell am I? Just what makes me the way I am?' No, me neither. But when old age came knocking on the door, I discovered my thoughts were dwelling more and more in the past rather than looking to the future. With this came the realisation that I knew very little about my kith and kin, the people who put me on this earth.

Funnily enough, it was the BBC's *Who Do You Think You Are?* that really galvanized my resolve, notably an edition featuring Kate Humble. The name Humble is very significant in Elm history; for many years my paternal grandparents were in service to a family of that name. But was it the same Humble family?

⊙⊙⊙

My paternal grandfather was a Yorkshireman, but only just in that he was born in the small town of Greenfield, perched high up on the moors and only a whisker on the right side of the border with the county about which no self-respecting Yorkshireman speaks: Lancashire. Sadly, it's all academic now because in 1974 local government reorganisation saw the area subsumed into the grey amorphous blob that became known as Greater Manchester, a fate compounded some twelve years later when governance was transferred to Oldham Metropolitan Borough Council.

Anyway, back in those heady old Yorkshire years, my grandfather Harry was born to Elijah, a policeman, and Henrietta. I take great pride in mentioning her on account of her trade; she was a woollen-hat hardener, an occupation guaranteed to confound the panel of *What's My Line?* For the benefit of readers not yet drawing their pension, that was a TV game show where a team of celebrities had to guess the profession or trade of someone based on a piece of mime performed by the contestant. Bricklayer – easy; bell-ringer – piece of cake; barmaid – doddle; woollen-hat hardener – er, I don't think so!

Some years later, the family moved to the tiny village of Burghwallis, about six miles north of Doncaster. Here my grandfather was eventually employed as a surface worker at a nearby colliery. His ability to drive, something he had been encouraged to do by a previous employer, drew the attention of the pit owner who required the services of a chauffeur. That person was William Humble who was, I'm pleased to tell you, great-grandfather to TV presenter Kate. Mystery solved!

In 1913, Harry caught the eye of Lincolnshire lass Hilda Joynes, who was in domestic service to a family at nearby Skellow Grange. They married in June the following year before Harry ventured forth to fight for king and country.

You may be familiar with the Joynes family, or at least my great-uncle Richard 'Dickie' Joynes. No? Well, you might be if you'd been reading the back page of your Sunday paper on the morning of 7th of September 1902, because the previous day he scored in Notts County's 3–1 defeat of West Bromwich Albion. Back then, this was England's top-flight league (today's premiership).

I have a team photograph depicting Dickie sporting a luxuriant moustache and looking as if he'd be more comfortable in a barber's shop quartet. Fashions may have changed but, given the exaggerated status afforded to professional footballers these days, I'm sure he was considered to be a household name of his time.

Anyway, I digress.

The final piece of the Elm/Humble jigsaw fell into place sometime after the war when the Humble family moved to Skellow Grange and a new period began in the lives of Harry and Hilda. Now in the company of Harry's mother, Henrietta, who had been widowed by the premature death of Elijah, they moved into a little lodge on the Skellow Grange estate where all three found themselves in domestic service to the Humbles. It was an association that saw the two families intertwined for about forty years until the death of William Humble in 1964.

It is my belief that the families were, in their own ways, mutually supportive. My grandfather's association with Mr Humble became more and more symbiotic as they grew old together.

I am a landscape architect, so you will appreciate how happy I was to discover links, however tenuous, between my maternal family and Gertrude Jekyll, the eminent turn-of-the-century garden designer. Let me explain.

It seems that Miss Jekyll, along with Rudyard Kipling, was a close friend of a gentleman with the rather grand name of Hercules Brabazon-Brabazon, the owner of Oaklands, a vast, rambling, country estate in East Sussex. There, amongst Mr B-B's domestic staff, we find my maternal grandfather, a coachman by the name of Samuel Coleman. It is highly likely he was responsible for transporting Mr B-B's visitors and house guests, so there is a very real possibility that my grandfather encountered and conversed with Miss Jekyll.

So what, I hear you say. Well, let me tell you this: in the small, insular world of landscape architects and garden designers, a connection of this significance, albeit unsubstantiated, cannot be overstated. It makes me pretty much horticultural royalty!

How any conversation between them might have progressed is anyone's guess, given that my grandfather was rather deaf and Miss Jekyll's eyesight was less than perfect. Did it actually happen? Who knows? I'm going to believe it did; for me, it is an image to be cherished.

History suggests that Samuel encountered his wife-to-be, Gertrude Pauling, whilst working at Oaklands. It remains unclear how this came about, given that her family roots were some two hundred miles away in Derby where she grew up as one of thirteen children born to a master baker.

As it turned out, their association with Oaklands was not a particularly lengthy one because in 1906 Brabazon-Brabazon passed away. This prompted major changes on the estate, not least of which was a significant reduction in staff. Given the arrival of the internal combustion engine, I imagine my coachman grandfather featured rather prominently on the redundancy list.

At the outbreak of WW1 they were in London, where Samuel was assigned to Woolwich Arsenal munitions factory having been rejected for military service on account of his deafness. When the war was over (and now with three children, the youngest of whom was my mother), they moved away from the capital to Hatfield in Hertfordshire.

Now, I should say a little about my maternal grandparents' home. To me as a child, living and enjoying the benefits of a relatively spacious new council house, their house seemed positively archaic, even if the technologies of coal fires and copper wash tubs were pretty much the same.

The substantial, defining difference for me were the bathroom facilities. As an old romantic, you might think a candlelit toilet was something I'd find agreeable – but not one in a freezing cold outhouse divided from the rest of the world by nothing more than an ill-fitting door. Also, not being an avid consumer of the written word, the prospect of being able to read the toilet paper before actually putting it to use was rather lost on me.

It's all relative, but without doubt my grandparents' house was a humble abode. The ground floor consisted of a front room, a dining/living room and a rudimentary kitchen, or 'scullery' as it was called. The scullery also housed a bath tub, screened from view by a curtain, an arrangement that has the potential for all manner of multi-tasking, none of which I'd like to believe ever happened! Upstairs was divided into three bedrooms and outside, in addition to the yard and privy, was my grandad's pigeon loft. Beyond that was a decent-sized, well-tended and productive garden.

The contents spanned a century of domesticity: heavy dark curtains hanging from stout wooden rings and poles; marble-topped wash stands; an art-deco soda syphon perched on the sideboard, and a radiogram the size of a starter home. An old oak grandfather clock ticked away the minutes, hours and years, witness to the tribulations of war, the daily humdrum of life, memories of Christmas sing-songs around an upright piano, and happy winter evenings playing parlour games in front of an open fire.

These were the memories of my forebears. However, having been taught some of those simple games such as Hunt the Thimble, I felt a tenuous connection with the history of that little terraced house.

Humble abode it may have been, but I am eternally grateful for its resilience. If Hitler's bomb aimers had strayed a degree or so, I might never have seen it or my grandparents. During two fateful days in the autumn of 1944, the town was hit by German (V1) flying bombs – doodlebugs. One exploded on the outskirts near the de Havilland airfield, killing four people, and a second just to the rear of my grandparents' home. This explosion killed another nine people and destroyed a school.

The structural damage to their cottage was such that the gable wall had to be shored up with a timber truss that spanned the gap to the next terrace, thus supporting both structures. That is how it remained until the late 1960s, when the local authority achieved what the Luftwaffe failed to do and demolished the lot to make way for offices and commercial premises. I'm sure their removal was lamented by some who had lived in these modest little cottages, but this was the genesis of a 'brave new world' in which sentiment would have little part to play.

I assume that the de Havilland aircraft factory and its adjoining airfield, founded in the thirties, was the reason for the Germans targeting the town. Prior to the war, the company had designed and manufactured the Tiger Moth biplane, much used by the RAF as a training aircraft. De Havilland's contribution to the war effort came in the form of the Mosquito, a fighter bomber which, despite a flimsy construction of timber and canvas, became a major part of the RAF's strike force.

The coming together of my parents was a classic, if not uncommon, wartime story of boy meets girl. My mother told me their first meeting happened on a railway station where she had agreed to chaperone a fellow Wren (Women's Royal Navy) who was there to see her RAF boyfriend. As I understand it, my father was the opposite number, the friend of the boyfriend. Letters were exchanged during the war but communications started to dry up as hostilities drew to a close. Then, whilst clearing out his kit bag somewhere in Europe, my father came across one of my mother's letters. He decided to write to her again and, as they say, the rest is history.

My father had an inauspicious start to life. Like his father before him, he worked in the offices of the local colliery until he volunteered to join the RAF during WW2. In the rank of wireless operator, he was amongst the second wave of troops sent in to drive back the Germans following the D-Day landings. He did his bit as many ordinary folk did; to this day I ask myself if I could have done the same.

He was a very able cricketer and a passable footballer, though I know his passion was for the former. I recall watching him play cricket when I was a kid and I remember him as an enthusiastic all-rounder, able to bowl fast left arm and also pretty handy with the bat with which, for some strange reason, he was right-handed.

My mother made her contribution to the war effort while serving at Bletchley Park with the codebreakers, though she never spoke about it until a few years prior to her death. '*I did a bit of typing,*' was her usual reply to any inquisitor. However, in recent years the Ministry of Defence released a 'roll of honour' naming all those who served at Bletchley Park and my mother is listed as a bombe-machine operator. That was the very machine designed from scratch by Alan Turing that is credited with shortening the war by two years and saving the lives of thousands of servicemen. The fact that my mother might have played even the smallest part in this is something in which I take great pride.

Like so many others, she took the order of secrecy required of those who served at Bletchley very seriously and remained resolute despite the passing years. Her natural modesty tended to belie her intelligence, though her ability to complete crosswords even into her nineties was a clear indication of an organised, agile mind.

Both my parents were brought up in families underpinned by Christian beliefs, and both shared a love of nature and a respect for the environment. They were down-to-earth, hard-working people who made the most of a post-war Britain that had few luxuries to offer. They went about life with good humour, supported their family and always set a good example. I am immensely proud of them.

I believe that my parentage made me a better person. I was able to enjoy the respective halves of the family and appreciate their backgrounds without the prejudice that often emerges when a family becomes polarised in one area and has no other points of reference. It is a family tree that includes men and women, some of whose lives span two world wars, who were imbued with the ethics, lifestyle and social history of a Victorian dynasty that fashioned society long after it had technically ceased to exist. On both sides the underlying theme was that of service, both military and domestic, and I am prepared to entertain the very real possibility that this dedication and loyalty has informed my own approach to discipline and behaviour. That said, there is absolutely nothing in my lineage that sheds any light on my career choice, a choice that was made at a very young age and without direction.

The chauffeur, the baker and secret codebreaker are all very interesting, but they sure as hell ain't me and are most certainly not in my psyche. For example, try as I might, I cannot match my mother's puzzle-solving abilities. Also, as far as I can remember, I've never looked at a woolly hat and thought, '*By 'eck, that could do with a good stiffening!*'

I believe there is something else that makes us all truly unique, but I think I'll leave that highly subjective debate to the whims and notions of the psychology wallahs.

O2

BOOMERSVILLE

SCRAPING shapes in the frost on the inside of my bedroom window is one of my earliest recollections of home life. That was pretty much par for the course in a post-war council house, central heating being the privilege of posh people who owned their own homes. But in the chill of post-war Britain, the daily routine for many was lighting a coal fire to warm and breathe life into the home.

Prime Minister Harold MacMillan was busy telling us '*You've never had it so good*' (not me obviously, as I was just a kid and couldn't give a monkey's). Set against the six years of wartime turmoil that had gone before, I guess that was an easy claim to make. However, there was a lot more to his rhetoric than afterglow, little of which had anything to do with the Conservative administration he presided over.

It was, in fact, previous Labour governments that had done much to ease the pain of the less fortunate by introducing a National Health Service and welfare state that gave new confidence to the post-war generation. But credit where credit's due: the MacMillan government was responsible for the building programme that delivered huge numbers of council houses, which meant that 'ordinary' families had decent, if not very exciting, places to call home. It was a situation arguably better than today, when the waiting time for social housing extends into infinity and private renting is being exploited by a new class of landlords, some of whom seem to approach the concept as a means of legalized extortion. I said I hoped to ruffle a few feathers, remember!

Home was Hatfield, where my mother had been brought up and where she and my father started their married life. We lived in an unexceptional council house in an unexceptional street, save for the fact that Mick Taylor, later to become a member of the Rolling Stones, lived about a hundred yards up the road. And from day one, I was not alone.

I had an elder brother three years my senior. His example has been a constant influence, not least because I ended up wearing his hand-me-down clothes until I was into my early teens, and he used to thrash me at any game or sport we played. Three years is a big difference, especially during the inevitable moments of sibling rivalry.

On the plus side, he bore the brunt of all the irksome parent–teenager conflicts that frequently revolved around clothing (particularly shoes), hair and the Rolling Stones. When I arrived at the tempestuous teens, it was as much as I could do to raise a disapproving tut for my selection of tangerine hipsters and Cuban-heeled, chisel-toed shoes! Ah, the sixties! How they are missed.

This unexceptional street, Lockley Crescent, lies within an area known as Birchwood at the northern edge of the town. A substantial part of Birchwood was developed by way of council housing immediately after the war. I suspect my mother's recollections of the fields and country lanes that were its former glory provoked mixed feelings about the new roof above her head; it would have been difficult not to have such nostalgic thoughts.

The sprawling web of interlocking crescents and avenues was mostly given over to semi-detached and terraced houses, but within its midst sat an estate made up entirely of temporary prefabricated bungalows. These were an essential part of the quick fix designed to overcome the severe housing shortage. I can't begin to imagine what convoluted lottery of local government decision-making processes went into determining why some folk were allocated brick-built homes and others these temporary dwellings, but it would be a while before the occupants of the latter were able to share the semi-detached suburban 'heaven' to which we had become accustomed.

Our little slice of this 'heaven' was about half way down the meandering crescent and nestled between two spacious greens, one often referred to as The Pan and the other rather less imaginatively called The Green. Given that sporting activities occupied pretty much all the hours of recreation my brother and I enjoyed, you'll understand the significance of these spaces in our early lives.

Our equipment was pretty rudimentary, but so was that of the men who played sport professionally at that time, most notably footballers. Football boots appeared to derive their design more from military or heavy industrial activities than any desire to allow Stanley Matthews to 'bend it like Beckham'. Brown thick-leather boots, fitted at the business end with wooden toecaps and provided with an undercarriage of nailed-in studs, were tied well above the ankle and secured with laces long enough to rig the *Cutty Sark*. The design of such heavy artillery in the foot department was not without reason. By mid-season the football pitches had generally taken on the appearance of ploughed fields, causing the highly absorbent ball to gain weight at an alarming rate. All very different to today, where balls have protective coatings, playing surfaces resemble bowling greens and footballers prance about in garish footwear that would look more appropriate on a catwalk!

Thinking back to this time and all the hours we spent running around on The Green and The Pan, did we ever realise how fortunate we were to have them? Why would we? To us they were merely random areas of grass with a few trees (goalposts), on which we could act out our footballing fantasies. But as I now know, their existence was rather more significant than that. The inclusion of such areas was symbolic of a new, more informed approach to the way we designed our towns and residential areas. Yes, the Victorians set out their parks, and yes, Ebenezer Howard had created a garden city format for Letchworth and nearby Welwyn Garden City, but this was a new beginning. Our estates were set out in accordance with design criteria for open space and living requirements, most notably detailed in documents such as the Parker Morris standards. This new thinking would shine no more brightly than in the 'new town' movement.

Hatfield was one of several towns in the south-east selected for expansion in accordance with this philosophy, taking folks from the slums of war-ravaged London and helping accommodate the baby boom that followed. Other completely new towns were developed to deal with these problems, most notably at Harlow, Stevenage and later Milton Keynes. Though I didn't know it at the time, two of these would play a significant part in my early working life and the new-town philosophy would be firmly instilled into my very being.

Before I regale you with the delights of my home town, I want to examine the expression 'baby boomers' because it defines my generation. I think this is important, especially as we boomers are now regarded as social pariahs for having the audacity to take our old-age pensions, thereby putting a strain on the national economy, not to mention the NHS. You might think that is an inevitable consequence of a spike in the population, but it is one that successive governments over the last fifty years have failed to see coming – or chosen to ignore.

I thought I'd do a bit of research on the subject. My probing, which lasted all of about ten minutes, turned up all sorts of sophisticated hypotheses, none of which seemed to have any grasp of human nature.

The general consensus suggests that rapid increases in population are linked to periods of economic and social stability. Post-war Britain in the 1950s was showing signs of recovery but times were still difficult, with food rationing continuing almost to the middle of the decade. I am not, therefore, entirely convinced by this theory.

I suggest that the spark that ignited the boom came a few years earlier and was rather more to do with base instincts and human nature than pounds in pockets. Remember that the population had just endured six years of war, during which time many had lived in constant fear for their lives, so it is not difficult to appreciate the sense of euphoria as hostilities ceased. I should imagine the now hackneyed anti-war slogan of the 1960s 'make love not war' had similar resonance some twenty years previously, so who could blame people for wanting to indulge in the pleasures of the bedroom?

The flames of passion were further fanned by a government policy that provided child allowance, but only for the second born. I guess it was very much a case of 'in for a penny, in for five bob', that being the weekly amount of the benefit. It is therefore something of an affront when our esteemed captains of government wag accusing fingers at us boomers for jeopardising the economy. It's really the fault of their predecessors – and the BBC. Why the BBC? Well, I suspect their tardiness in broadcasting during the immediate post-war years, and therefore the very limited sales of TVs, must have initiated many an early night of passion!

⊙⊙⊙

Hatfield lies about twenty miles due north of London and is, in the main, rather undistinguished, most of it being built in some haste after WW2. The old town is considerably more interesting. Its skyline is dominated by the parish church of St Etheldreda that dates back to the fifteenth century, behind which is the old Royal Palace and Hatfield House, the seat of the Salisbury family and one of the country's most visited stately homes.

Bradshaw's *Descriptive Railway Handbook* of 1863 says of Hatfield: *It is well known on account of the royal palace, which was for some time the residence of Queen Elizabeth, previous to the death of her sister Mary. Here is also the magnificent palace erected by Cecil, first Earl of Salisbury, which retains, to this day, nearly all its original splendour.*

This substantial, ornate edifice provided a stunning backdrop to the pitch of Hatfield Estate Cricket Club, upon which my father, my brother and I all had the good fortune to swing the willow. There could be fewer more picturesque venues; its manicured sward was set within verdant parkland, one boundary being defined by a majestic avenue of ancient lime trees. I find it sad that our memories will never be

16

experienced by later generations; the sound of willow on leather is no longer heard in that beautiful natural arena, and those balmy summer afternoons seem destined to be consigned to history.

In being mentioned in Bradshaw's *Handbook*, you will understand the significance of the railway to the recent history of the town. The east-coast line, constructed in the middle of the nineteenth century, linked London with York and Edinburgh; Hatfield featured as a regular stop on that itinerary. That status was lost back in the fifties and sixties when it was downgraded to deal only with suburban traffic to the City and link into other stations that provide connections to the wider network.

Despite this apparent decline, Hatfield station continued to be a busy place until being emasculated by root and branch changes in the 1970s that left it a shadow of its former self. The station I remember from my childhood was well appointed with several facilities including a bar, buffet, ladies' and general waiting rooms (both with roaring fires in winter), and the other rooms and offices associated with the hustle and bustle of an active railway station. The platforms were covered by a protective canopy over much of their length, a far cry from the miserable little shelters that have since replaced them. This retrogressive step has been repeated on many a station across the network where, it seems, customer welfare is of little concern compared to shareholder dividends. Indeed, it seems to have been downhill for the railways since that nasty Beeching chap stuck his nose in.

I have fond memories of being consumed by the steam, smoke and deafening sound of locomotives as they blasted along the platforms pulling long lines of carriages. Occasionally a Pullman-class train thundered through with its chocolate and cream livery, curtained windows and table lights shining seductively. It all looked so romantic and sophisticated, rather like something in a Jack Vettriano painting.

In addition to the passenger service, the station had a thriving goods depot. This included many sidings where scruffy little tank engines trundled up and down shunting trucks to form goods trains that carried merchandise to the far-flung corners of the region.

My brother and I had a superb vantage point from which to view the comings and goings because our grandparents' cottage was about fifty metres from the lines. Yes, you've guessed it: we were train-spotters.

It sounds very nerdy now but back then, other than activities that required a ball, train spotting was pretty much the number-one hobby. Just equip us with a copy of *Ian Allen's Loco Spotters*, a biro, a ruler and bar of Fry's Five Boys chocolate and we were happy for hours. Indeed we had many hours of enjoyment observing this ever-changing scene from my grandparents' bedroom window, though I know my grandmother did not share our pleasure, especially on wash days. There were many occasions when she hung out a line of whites only to have it immersed in a deluge of black smuts either from the coal-loading hopper or the smoke and steam snorting from the hard-working locomotives. This often resulted in a complete rewash before the clothes were put through the mangle that resided in the corner of the back yard and hung out again.

⊙⊙⊙

My dad worked in the offices of Jack Oldings, the town's largest employer after the de Havilland aircraft company. At the time it was part of Caterpillar Tractors, but after WW2 it transferred to the Vickers Group and became an agent for a new Vickers' tractor.

I believe that this Rolls-Royce powered vehicle, known as the Vigor, was based on technology garnered during the war when the company was adapting machines to assist with the deployment of troops, notably at the D-Day landings. Sadly, the vehicle that helped push back the Nazi war machine did not adapt too well to peace-time duties and this, plus severe competition from Caterpillar, meant that the project was short lived. Nevertheless, the company continued to operate for many years in the business of earth-moving equipment through a series of changes, franchises and take-overs.

Its premises were on the northernmost edge of the town. Much of the site was covered with vast sheds where the business of repairing and servicing these temperamental earth-moving leviathans was carried out. At its most prominent point, facing the A1, the company had rather fine art-deco offices, the centrepiece of which was a magnificent clock tower complete with flagpole flying the company's blue triangular pennant. It was an impressive landmark and made, I felt, a positive and totally identifiable statement about Hatfield.

Unfortunately, this unique and substantial building was swept away in 1986 to be replaced by Tesco and Habitat, etc., whose mundane structures offer nothing to the landscape and are commonplace across the country. The 1930s offices at the de Havilland factory were later spared a similar fate and re-purposed as a police station/courtroom complex.

My parents, like so many other young couples of the time, had very little and I'm pretty sure my father's early income from Jack Oldings was quite modest. Most of our household furnishings were second hand, though we did have a television. I don't know where the set came from, but I do recall my dad spending quite a lot of time fiddling with its inner workings to stop the picture rolling or to deliver an image through a screen of TV snow.

With no refrigerator, and in a world not yet riddled with preservatives, fast food and E numbers, my mother was constantly out buying fresh groceries for meals that were presented pretty much on the basis of 'take it or leave it'. Nevertheless our post-war diet, basic as it may have been, was quite nutritious, and was supplemented by produce from a decent-sized garden that served the family well. In the 1950s the idea of 'digging for victory' still resonated and many people, my folks included, continued to grow their own fruit and vegetables.

Microwave ovens, TV dinners and boil-in-a bag food didn't exist; it was still some time before our high streets would become lined with Indian and Chinese takeaways, kebab houses and burger joints. In fact there were very few restaurants at all; the only notable distractions from a rather repetitive diet were the occasional fish-and-chip suppers and tinned fruit salad on a Sunday.

Did we feel deprived? No, of course we didn't. We knew nothing else. Although it is a parody, The Scaffold song of 1966, '2 Days Monday', sums things up in its description of working-class diets and domesticity. As we now confront the serious problem of obesity, aided and abetted by companies telling us to '*just eat*', those words from The Scaffold seem to echo with a comforting, wholesome, healthy feeling of nostalgia.

Prior to the 1960s, when Hatfield's new shopping centre opened, all food and household goods were provided by an array of traders centred on Old Hatfield, though several small parades of shops served other areas. The Co-op was the only place that resembled a supermarket in that it sold a variety of goods – but even that was little more than a glorified version of Arkwright's shop in *Open all Hours*.

There were a number of mobile traders peddling their wares from vans and carts to supplement any shortfall. These included a fishmonger, a general grocer, and a greengrocer who travelled down from the market gardens of Sandy in Bedfordshire. Every Saturday he sold produce from the back of a truck that looked every bit as if it had driven out of a scene from *The Beverly Hillbillies*. The greengrocer himself looked like a member of the cast.

Then there was our wonderful milkman, a true giant amongst tradesmen. Clad in a brown storekeeper's coat, with an old leather money bag slung over his shoulder, he delivered his gold and silver tops to our doorsteps through thick and thin, rain or shine. His methodology was faultless; whilst he strode briskly down the street from cart to doorstep with full bottles and back with the empties, his trusty horse pulled the cart along at an appropriate pace.

It was a perfectly synchronised, efficient and environmentally friendly system. Occasionally the milkman paused outside our garden to give his horse a feed bag, during which time it regularly deposited a heap of steaming crap. That wasn't a problem during the winter months but a bit of a bugger in the summer because this particular section of road constituted the Wimbledon centre court, as played on by my brother and me. Still, our loss was very much our neighbour's gain, and he was quick to add some value to his compost heap and ultimately his rose bushes.

We baby boomers were born to a nation in the aftermath of world war. It was a time of austerity and making do, but I do not feel a sad violin lament washing over me as I write. That is because it was also a time of simplicity and fresh hope, of community and greater environmental stability. Obviously we were unaware of our good fortune at the time; such feelings are rooted in hindsight, and it is only by looking at the challenges facing kids today that I can truly appreciate my childhood.

And, talking of violins...

03

THE VIOLIN YEARS

WEEKDAYS began early with a couple of miles' walk or cycle. It's hard to believe that I actually used to cross the A1 to go to school. Back then it was only a single carriageway and traffic levels were not exactly a threat to the ozone layer, but it was still a pretty astonishing feat. My friend, Ian, used to cross at a different location about half a mile away, aided by the caretaker/lollie pop man. Yes, a lollie pop man on the A1!

Having navigated the crossing, I was left to cycle the remainder of the journey on my green Raleigh Space Rider, violin case clattering against my knee and front forks. This last phase of the journey took me across a farm track, and I believe this is where I first started to develop an awareness and love for the environment. The track had three trees spaced along its arrow-straight path: a couple of oaks with a magnificent mature elm in the middle. I remember passing the farmer who was sitting on the front wheel of his tractor, breakfast sandwich in hand, surrounded by the smell of newly turned soil and diesel, and the sound of an ascending skylark in a topaz-blue sky. A really heady combination: moist, rich, brown earth, National Benzole and just a hint of Vaughan-Williams!

It was a good place to go to school, located on the very edge of the town with de Havilland airfield close. Here the Comet, the world's first jet airliner, was in production, soon to be followed by its successor, the Trident. Elsewhere the school was surrounded by a broad expanse of hedge-lined fields and occasional trees, which featured prominently in the nature walks that were a regular part of our lessons.

We learnt about crop rotation and some rudimentary plant physiology; I distinctly remember being shown the flower and subsequent seed of the aforementioned elm tree. I probably thought it had been there since time immemorial and would remain there for ever, but it succumbed to Dutch elm disease like so many others and was gone within twenty years. I suspect it was my first experience of our dynamic, constantly changing environment, though it would be a while before I started to appreciate the complexities of nature and ecology.

Apart from the traditional 3 Rs-based curriculum, the school had a very strong leaning toward the arts, which suited me fine as I was not a very academic child. The headmaster was a kindly man, generous of spirit and very much a teacher of the old school. He seemed most happy when chipping in with some of the teaching, and liked nothing better than rolling up his sleeves and taking a pottery class. Music also featured heavily; in the early years this involved little more than clattering percussion instruments, but later we were taught the recorder and, for the more ambitious (or in my case overly optimistic), the violin.

Given this background, it is perhaps not surprising that the school produced more than its fair share of musical talent. Colin Blunstone, lead singer of The Zombies, was a pupil there several years ahead of me. If you're about my age, I'm sure you will remember their song 'She's Not There', which was a hit on both sides of the Atlantic in 1964, making number one in the US. You might also recall some of his songs as a solo performer, 'Say You Don't Mind' and 'I Don't Believe In Miracles' being most memorable in a career that has spanned pretty much six decades.

In the same class as me was the enigmatic Barbara Gaskin. Well, not particularly enigmatic at nine years of age – that came later. Her chart-topping hit, a cover version of 'It's My Party (And I'll Cry If I Want To)', was the means by which she entered the exclusive, yet strangely infamous, club of one-hit wonders.

⊙ ⊙ ⊙

The school was Green Lanes Junior Mixed Infants. A sturdy, traditional red-brick structure with cricket stumps painted on the front gable end to facilitate hours of playtime practice for the up-and-coming Ben Stokeses (or Ted Dexters as we called them back then).

The main classrooms ran east to west facing the school field to the south, so on bright summer days the sun poured through the tall, multi-paned classroom windows. A long corridor ran the length of the building separating the classrooms from the assembly hall. Each side of that, and again separated by corridors, was a cloakroom; both were entered via two wide archways that gave them a cloister-like feel.

These cloakrooms played host to the occasional visit of the nit nurse, whose sole purpose in life seemed to be to ruffle our barnets to see what wildlife she might dislodge, rather like the apes you see in David Attenborough documentaries. She only differed from them in that she chose, quite wisely in my opinion, not to eat any organism that she flushed out with her probing.

There were more rooms above each cloakroom, accessed by highly polished wooden stairs. Above the junior cloakroom was the school library which, in doubling as the staff room, frequently emitted an aroma of sweet coffee. Next to that was Miss Wells' classroom; I later found out that she was a descendant of HG. I was never actually taught by Miss Wells, which probably explains my woefully poor knowledge of English literature. Above the senior cloakroom was a similar arrangement of rooms, including the headmaster's study, secretary's office and a classroom that saw only occasional use but which doubled as the venue for my violin lessons.

The shape and orientation of the building divided the playground into three separate areas, the central one being flanked on three sides by heavily glazed walls, so not conducive to ball games. The western playground separated the school building from the canteen where I enjoyed many a good meal, contrary to the popularly held schoolboy stereotype.

This was the junior end of the establishment where we had outdoor PE, which usually involved throwing things such as old sorbo rubber balls (whose original spongey consistency had, over many years, turned to what seemed like an amalgam of latex and lead), and grubby, hand-stitched bean bags. Cane hoola-hoops also featured in our PE routines though, as a slightly chubby child, I can't imagine they had too much appeal.

And here I really must mention Miss Hill, my first teacher in class one, or the reception class as it is often called today. I don't know if it was simply because this was the first time I had been away from my mother's side, but I felt an attraction toward Miss Hill that was strange and mysterious yet, at the same time, rather pleasing.

Our school days were articulated by three breaks: morning and afternoon playtimes, and lunch. And if you are more than fifty years old, you will probably be familiar with the concept of school milk, which was delivered in strange little bottles holding a third of a pint. Drinking this during the morning playtime was pretty much compulsory. That was all fine and dandy during temperate weather, but during winter the milk often solidified into a block of ice and in summer, having spent an hour or so sitting in the sun, it was pretty much a sandwich filler rather than a drink!

Throughout the winter, every break was consumed by football matches. Our pitch was the eastern playground at the front of the school. One goal was the gable end of the bike shed, defined by a strategically placed drainpipe and a substantial concrete bollard, and the other was between a silver birch tree and a small lilac bush. The horticultural end was the favoured end because it was on a small area of grass rather than tarmacadam. This gave goalkeepers the opportunity to pull off ambitious diving saves that would have been sheer folly at the shed end.

Each match was preceded by the ritual of stone, paper, scissors, to establish who had first dibs on team selection. If it was my turn to hold that privileged position, I always made sure I picked my mate, Ian. He was a slight kid with skinny little legs, brown curly hair and circular horn-rimmed spectacles, an appearance that undersold his footballing skills. Put a tennis ball at his feet and he became Maradona. No, forget

25

that: he was far better because, unlike Maradona, he had to contend with the swarm, the swarm being every other participant in the game who chased after the ball like iron filings to a magnet. There was also the additional hazard of innocent bystanders to deal with. Once in possession of the ball, Ian would set off like a startled jack rabbit, jinking in and out of the mêlée on ambitious dribbles that might take him around the playground several times before he could break free and ping a shot with pinpoint accuracy against the bike-shed wall.

⊙ ⊙ ⊙

In addition to sport, popular music was starting to demand our attention. At this time, it was undergoing a massive cultural and generational transformation that was apparent even to kids of our tender years. The US had jettisoned the big-band swing era, synonymous with wartime films, and was replacing it with rockabilly and then rock 'n' roll, often referred to as the devil's music. This radically new sound, with its roots in blues and country music, was quickly absorbed into the psyche of Britain's youth and it conquered our music charts.

My earliest recollection of the devil's music was at a travelling fair that pitched up once a year on wasteland near my home, its PA system straining to lift the sounds of Buddy Holly, Elvis Presley, Eddie Cochran and Del Shannon above the hum and clatter of the fairground noise.

That sound would become erroneously associated with a social subculture in the UK, known as 'Teddy Boys'. Their style being loosely based on the concept of the British dandy: drape coats, drainpipe trousers and suede 'brothel-creeper' shoes. Throughout the mid to late fifties they earned a slightly menacing reputation, in marked contrast to their style icons of the past.

American country, blues and jazz conspired in the creation of skiffle, which had the added attraction of being playable on improvised or homemade instruments; at a time of economic constraint, that made it more accessible for would-be musicians. It was a style championed in the UK by Lonnie Donegan, earning him the title 'King of Skiffle'. I didn't really get it; a Scottish Cockney singing American songs like 'Rock Island Line' and 'Gamblin' Man' seemed rather bizarre to me – and still does.

Jazz was also lost on me, both the brassy wah-wah Dixieland trad and the self-indulgent, tuneless, plinky-plink piano, drums and bass stuff. These were curious bedfellows loosely covered by the term 'beat', and gave rise to the fifties' beatniks. This subculture appeared to align itself notionally with anarchic tendencies, but more than anything the term was a useful condemnation for pretty much anyone who didn't conform to the perceived norms of the time.

The beatniks were curious souls, frequently overwhelmed by an irresistible urge to grow beards (obviously just the men), don black berets and black polo-neck sweaters, and buy themselves a set of bongos.

As a junior-school innocent, I had no understanding of these trends, other than knowing never to piss off a Teddy Boy. I did buy seven-inch singles by several American singers and their British imitators, but these were a temporary aside until my eyes and ears were regaled by the wonderful era of pop and rock music that was to play such a large role in my teens and later life. Only then did I understand how all these interventions had helped to sculpt the musical landscape of my generation, so my thanks to you all – even Lonnie!

As for the violin...

For several years I scraped and scratched the fiddle under the tutelage of an ageing, rather irascible gentleman by the name of Gasparyan who, judging from his thick accent, hailed from some part of eastern Europe. He used to beat time with a thunderous stamping of his foot that echoed through the school corridors, occasionally accompanying this with an operatic bellow of '*Up zee violin*' if he noticed our shoulders drooping under the strain. It was, however, a lost cause; I knew that somehow I had to confront my folks with the possibility I might not be the next Yehudi Menuhin.

This was a brave move on my part; Mum's side of the family was pretty musical so I expected to be given a hard time. As it turned out, I think they were very close to making the first move because of the terrible noise I'd been generating! I still don't understand how a violin in the hands of Nigel Kennedy, Nicola Benedetti or Dave Swarbrick can send shivers down the spine when all I could do was squeak and scrape.

04

FIFTEEN QUID LEGENDS

ON 6th February 1958, Britain awoke to the sad news that many Manchester United footballers had perished in an air crash at Munich Airport. That made for a very sombre day at school, even amongst a group of eight- and nine-year-old kids. Many of those lost were little more than kids themselves, part of the celebrated Busby Babes put together by Matt Busby via the club's forward-thinking youth policy. It was an utter tragedy.

The silver lining to that sad day happened some ten years later, on the 29th of May 1968, when Manchester United became the first English club to win the European Cup. For those survivors of the air crash, namely Bobby Charlton, Bill Foulkes and manager Matt Busby, the moment must have been filled with a whole jumble of emotions. Bobby Charlton, in his book *My Life in Football*, described those moments:

There was absolutely no need for words. It had been his (Matt Busby) pioneering team that had been devastated on the European trail, and this was their symbolic rebirth. Tears were shed and nothing could bring back the lives that had been lost, but here, at least, was some sort of balance, perhaps even a degree of closure. Somehow Munich would have had a different significance for Manchester United if we hadn't won at Wembley on that tumultuous night in May 1968.

I think that, for one night at least, we were all Manchester United fans.

But I'm not going to go all dewy-eyed and tell you that the intervening ten years was a golden age of football, or some such cobblers. It was, in fact, a period of great change within the sport – and not always for the better.

My recollections began in February 1959 when my father took me to see my first professional match: Arsenal versus Portsmouth at Highbury. Jimmy Dickenson, the Portsmouth captain, was on his way to clocking up a total of 845 appearances for his club and had already won 48 caps representing his country, a truly remarkable achievement considering that far fewer international matches were played at that time. Being just a kid, I didn't understand the significance of this; I certainly didn't realise that I was watching pretty much the end of an era.

It was the start of the end of footballing innocence when professional footballers were ordinary working people venerated in their local communities purely because of their sporting skills. There seemed to be a parochial loyalty that bound player and fan together, a social linkage that transcended pitch and terrace; that was not particularly surprising when you consider that many footballers retained other jobs outside the sport in order to supplement their income. Stanley Mathews, unquestionably one of our greatest-ever players, ran a small hotel in Blackpool for many years; Tom Finney, another giant of the post-war era, continued to run a plumbing business, giving rise to his nickname 'The Preston Plumber', a term that was used even when he was a regular England international.

I'm sure that footballers of this period were less fit, slower and probably less skilful than their successors, but the question remains: did they provide less entertainment? I don't think so.

These were glory days for the spectator, but for the players it was another story. For as long as the game had been played professionally, the Football Association (with compliance from the clubs) had taken advantage of the men playing the game with restrictive practices, setting maximum weekly wages and tying players to clubs with contracts that gave them few rights. That had to change.

In 1961, George Eastham (all-round good guy, member of England's 1966 World Cup squad and the only signatory to my underused autograph book) went to court to challenge the stranglehold of the clubs. He won and the maximum wage was immediately abolished, but at the time he couldn't possibly have known the enormity of what he had unleashed.

At the start of the sixties, the average footballer's wage was about £15 per week but within a few years Johnny Haynes of Fulham was being paid £100 a week. Since then, the graph line plotting the increase in wages has risen steeply to such an extent that we have arrived at the opposite extreme. Players have become grossly overpaid in a sport that has become elitist and bloated by an avalanche of corporate funding, revenue from advertising and unrealistic deals associated with TV rights.

Gary Imlach, writer, TV commentator and son of 1959 FA Cup hero Stewart Imlach, writes in his excellent book *My Father and Other Working-Class Football Heroes*:

Football was a game of the working class, for the working class, by the working class. One thing it wasn't was a golden passport out of the working class.

But with the creation of the Premier League in 1992, just thirty years after the abolition of the maximum wage, a golden passport is exactly what the game has become for some. True, the stadiums have benefited greatly by the injection of finance, but the massive increase in the price of match tickets has become prohibitive to many of the people who made the game what it is – the working-class, grass-roots supporters.

Happily, back in November 1964 one such young supporter and a few of his school mates from Hatfield were able to find the few shillings necessary to get through the turnstiles and on to the terraces of Arsenal's Highbury Stadium. There, along with 59,636 others, he watched in awe a Manchester United forward line that included Bobby Charlton, Dennis Law and a young lad by the name of George Best, the trio that would later become known as the Manchester United Trinity.

The issues associated with football seem to embody much of what has occurred within society over the period of my lifetime: the triumph of celebrity and money over substance and value. I believe this is unsustainable and, given the clubs over-dependency on the continuation of this gravy train, I suspect it's only a matter of time before the whole thing goes belly-up.

We'll never see the likes again of a premiership 'Preston Plumber', but somewhere along the line there has to be a recalibration. If not, I suspect those that have been disenfranchised might well go looking for their pound of flesh and the return of their birthright.

I think it only fitting that a player should have the last word. In his autobiography, *The Ghost of '66*, Martin Peters wrote of his West Ham and England colleague Bobby Moore:

Bobby Moore was an iconic figure in the sixties. The captain of England, he stood astride the world game alongside Pele. Unlike David Beckham today, his fame was based almost solely on his ability to play football superbly well. Beckham plays football well, but his fame and popularity are due in no small part to the power of television, self-promotion, his pop star wife Victoria and the work of agents and publicists.

05

HIGH DAYS AND HOLIDAYS

LIFE was simple in post-war Britain and the hopes of council estate kids relatively modest, but come birthdays and Christmas my brother and I dared to have more ambitious expectations. I always enjoyed the sense of family occasion that came with such times, though my abiding memories of childhood birthday parties are of the sandwiches (usually egg or banana – ugh!), butterfly cakes and jelly, rather than the games and social interaction. I was clearly destined to be a kitchen dweller rather than a party animal.

The party games I do recall – and loathed – included Musical Chairs, Pass the Parcel and Pin the Tail on the Donkey and, if outdoor games were an option, Hide and Seek. Rather more obscure games, of which I am pleased to have little recollection of their rules or purpose, are the bizarrely named Squeak Piggy Squeak, Blind Man's Buff, and What's the Time, Mr Wolf?

And if the joys of such games were lost on *me* back in the fifties, imagine how today's six and seven year olds would react to them. How on earth did we get from Squeak Piggy Squeak to Wii, Play Stations and Xboxes in little more than half a century? On the plus side, back in those days we were more inclined to talk face to face, a rather more sociable and rewarding activity than Titter and Faceless Book.

Christmas remained a very special time for my brother and me. Today Christmas-themed paraphernalia appears in shops round about the same time the kids go back to school after the summer holiday, but for us it didn't really get started until a week or so into December. There were no artificial trees, so if you bought a Christmas tree any earlier you'd be up to your armpits in spruce needles before the first strains of 'We Wish you a Merry Christmas' reverberated tunelessly through your letter box.

To my mind, the amount of festive stuff that hits the shelves these days is rather disturbing and wasteful of material resources. I know this is going to sound cheesy but Christmas was more about seasonal and family tradition when I was a child. I enjoyed receiving gifts but I also enjoyed the security and comfort of the family unit, and Christmas was a time when the bonds that kept us close were made even stronger.

I remember two special Christmas occasions. The first heralded the arrival of a Hornby 00 train set; the second, several years later, brought a record player and signalled the end of the line for Tommy Steele 'Singing the Blues' via a wind-up gramophone.

The Phillips Disc Jockey Junior was a modest little piece of kit covered in grey Fablon and equipped with the most basic of mono-sound systems, but it was a passport to my musical future. Along with it came a selection of seven-inch singles that my brother and I felt compelled to play at about 7.00am on Christmas morning, something that, not surprisingly, didn't go down too well with the rest of the Elm household!

As summer approached the family's thoughts turned to holidays, which were usually taken at the Whitsuntide half-term break. I believe my parents opted for this time to avoid the crowds that flocked to the beaches prior to the advent of cheap package holidays to Spain.

My earliest holiday memory is of a place called Hunstanton on the Norfolk coast. Being only four or five at the time, I remember very little of it – though I seem to recall being frozen by the icy blast of an onshore wind rattling in from The Wash that could have blown the snow off an igloo. We have a solitary photograph of that time showing the family walking along the seafront clad in overcoats.

Holland-on-Sea near Clacton was our destination for the next couple of years. Again I remember the weather – constant sea mist – and the resounding bellow of a fog horn. Were we deterred from enjoying ourselves? The hell we were. We were down on the beach come what may, building vast sand castles and rushing to and from the sea with buckets of water to fill the surrounding moats, even though it soaked away into the sand quicker than we could fetch it. Then we splashed about in the sea until the integrity of our hand-knitted woollen bathing trunks became seriously compromised.

A weary walk home for tea, then out again to Clacton pier and the amusement arcade, where you could invest a penny in the sure and absolute certainty you would lose it. There were Spin-a-Win machines, where you pinged a ball bearing round a vertical spiral and watched it miss the holes marked 'Free Spin', only to see it fall through the one marked 'Lose'. There were machines where pennies deposited by the previous 950 losers stacked up on the brink of an oscillating surface; all you needed to do was roll another penny down a chute to dislodge £3 19s 2d worth of coppers into your lap. It never happened though, did it? And let's not forget the phone-box sized cabinet stuffed with sweets and cuddly toys, above which hung a mechanical grab that you manoeuvred with a joystick in order to lock its jaws onto your favourite piece of confectionery. It was funny how it always seemed to suffer an arthritic spasm just as you were about to liberate a Mars bar that had been incarcerated there since the end of the war.

In later years, my family travelled to more exotic holiday destinations in Devon and Wales. By this time, my brother and I were sports mad and spent hours on sandy beaches playing cricket or football with our father until the section of beach that constituted the pitch resembled a battlefield. Meanwhile, Mum used the time to relax, read the paper and simply observe all that was going on around her. My recollections here are of sunnier times, so it would appear that taking an early holiday was more often than not smiled upon by the weather gods.

Inevitably these family holidays came to an end. That happened in the mid-sixties when my brother turned eighteen and vetoed my parents' plans for any further family excursions. I joined them for one final fling to Scarborough, but it was all becoming a bit Alan Bennett by then.

We stayed in a 'respectable' B&B rather than self-catering as we usually did. The place was spotless, with an all-pervading aroma of canned fresh air. You could have eaten your breakfast off the toilet seat, something I considered doing rather than face the uninviting museum-like hush of the dining room, which was disturbed only by the scrape of gleaming cutlery upon floral-patterned plates and the occasional slurp of Maxwell House.

For a week we did what people did back then when holidaying in Scarborough. Dad and I played putting in Peasholm Park while Mum knitted; we watched the miniature naval warfare event (also in Peasholm Park) while Mum knitted; we played putting at the South Bay while Mum knitted, and we ventured out onto the North Yorkshire Moors – where Mum knitted.

'*Now then, John, how about a live show?*' Dad asked.

I was given a choice: Max Jaffa in his umpteenth season at the Spa, or a variety show at the Floral Hall. Mr Jaffa had been doing summer seasons at Scarborough for a hell of a long time; in fact, some say that his first show at the Spa was disrupted when a longboat sailed into the harbour and the theatre was ransacked by marauding Vikings.

'*Tell you what, Dad, let's do the variety show.*'

I seem to recall it featured local comedian Bobby Pattinson, crooner Jimmy Young and a Scottish vocal trio of triplet girls called The Karlins, who had enjoyed some recording success. Sadly, Scarborough Council saw fit to demolish the Floral Hall back in 1989, and I was very sorry to see that one of the Karlin girls recently succumbed to breast cancer. May you rest in peace, Linda, and thanks to you and your sisters for saving me from an evening of Max fiddlin' Jaffa!

⊙ ⊙ ⊙

We spent other holidays visiting my father's side of the family, just north of Doncaster. It was a long but simple journey almost entirely on the A1, which goes through Hatfield. Some 150 miles to the north, it also passes the end of the leafy lane where my grandparents lived.

Today this route can be driven relatively quickly, but in the early sixties the A1 threaded its way through all the towns en route so there was always a chance of a major hold-up. The beautiful town of Stamford was a case in point; its quaint, medieval road layout was more suited to hand carts and horse-drawn vehicles than cars and trucks. Doncaster was also frequently congested especially on race days, the town being synonymous with the St Leger, and it could take up to an hour to emerge over the town's North Bridge that spanned the River Don. Its murky black waters were often topped with a froth of filthy foam, a stark reminder of the region's industrial heritage. A far cry from leafy Hertfordshire.

It was always good to meet up with the northern half of the family. By this time my grandparents had moved out of the lodge and into a semi-detached stone cottage, though they were still on the estate where my grandfather remained a loyal employee of the Humble family. The other half of the semi was home to the McMartins, the estate gardener and his wife, affectionately known to us all as Uncle and Auntie Mac. Like most families, ours benefited from a whole raft of non-related members and the McMartins were, by now, ex-officio members to two generations of Elms.

I have fond memories of Uncle Mac. He was one of those archetypal figures you find in old photographs from the turn of the century until the 1920s in his collarless shirt, waistcoat, and with a Poirot-esque waxed moustache. He was a gentle, avuncular character with a lilting Scottish accent that sounded like a bumble bee singing a love song. Everything about him appealed to me – his kindly manner, his romantic appearance and, best of all, the environment in which he worked. The protected walled garden and glasshouses, laden with the sweet smell of heavy moist air, seemed very seductive. I can't think why they should have appealed to a young child but they did; had they been my destiny back in 1920, I'd have willingly taken it.

More family members lived a few hundred yards up the lane, and our cousin often joined my brother and me in games of cricket in the field behind our grandparents' cottage. These were very happy days spent running in the gentle green parkland and the company of the extended Elm Family.

I didn't appreciate it at the time, but I now realise it was something of a privileged existence. Bullcroft Colliery loomed large over the nearby village of Skellow about half a mile away, its slag heap and grimy streets a stark reminder of the hardship that many local families had endured for generations. That has all changed now: the shafts have been filled in and the slag heaps reshaped into grassy green mounds, all of which has substantially improved the local environment.

As a landscape architect I take some pride in this achievement, but there was a social and economic price that was paid by the hard-working people of these communities who lost their livelihood. Although the need to find alternatives to fossil fuels was inescapable, UK administrations made little attempt to manage the decline of deep-mine pits. Eventually that led to an unholy war between the government and the unions, something that would feature more prominently some years down the line.

06

LESSONS TO LEARN

MY junior years ended on something of a downer when I failed my eleven-plus examination. It was no great surprise; I lacked confidence and was painstakingly slow at pretty well everything – a late developer.

Three years earlier my brother had been more successful and was now at a local grammar school. If my folks were disappointed by my failure, they didn't show it. I recall my father saying, '*You're better off at the top of a secondary school than at the bottom of a grammar.*' Even at the tender age of eleven I found that a very positive and helpful attitude. It was little more than a chance comment, but it stayed with me and shaped my attitude for the rest of my school life.

My choice of school was relatively straightforward because there were just two local secondary moderns: Burleigh, a modern school built to serve the new town's expansion which had acquired a fairly disreputable reputation during its relatively short existence, or Onslow School which had no reputation at all because it didn't actually exist. It had previously been a joint grammar/secondary modern but, due to changes in the local education system, was going forward only as a secondary modern. The old school was being closed down and its replacement, about half a mile away, consisted of little more than a building site. My parents opted for the building site.

On a sunny autumn morning I dutifully – and very nervously – turned up for my first day of secondary education, only to find that two buildings of the three-block complex were far from completion. Transition from a cosy rural school to a big noisy secondary is tough as I recalled some thirty-six years later when my daughter made a similar move; being confronted with this state of affairs made it all the more challenging.

To overcome the problem, the old facility was kept open and the pupils had to commute from one to the other. The concept of moving between lessons was completely different to anything I had experienced previously, and travelling between schools was totally alien. When you consider the fortress-like fences and security systems that now protect our schools, it's hard to believe that we did this on a regular basis without any form of escort throughout the first year.

Notwithstanding these complications, I managed to settle in. After the initial filtering process, I found myself in the B stream, which was okay for starters. I made new friends quite well and things were fine for the first couple of years.

But the middle years were rather less happy. The onset of puberty is a difficult time for both sexes, with all the mood swings and tantrums, not to mention all the stuff that's going on with your body. Within my school year group it spawned a disruptive element which rather destabilized a hitherto friendly and relatively cohesive class.

Our form teacher/English teacher at that particular time, a lady by the name of Mrs Tyszka, was, like many of her colleagues, quite young and I suspect not greatly experienced. Add to that her diminutive stature, and it was easy to see how she might have felt intimidated by a bunch of rowdy, pimply lads, most of whom towered over her. Thinking back, I seem to recall she held her own pretty well; in any case, she looked damned attractive when she was angry, a fact that did not go unnoticed by *this* adolescent youth! (Memo to Miss Hill, Class 1, Green Lanes School: Consider yourself dumped – I have a new crush!)

Clearly this troublesome bunch had an agenda very different to mine in that they considered their education to be a trial and were intent on leaving school as quickly as possible. My agenda, on the other hand,

40

was to redeem myself from eleven-plus failure and to gain some O levels, perhaps even A levels, for no reason at this particular time other than for my own self-esteem.

For the next couple of years I found myself the butt of ridicule and, being so self-conscious, I was ill-equipped to deal with the situation. It was nothing like the horrific bullying stories we hear about today but more a case of prolonged peer-pressure intimidation. I don't think it actually affected my progress; in fact, I went on to pursue my personal scholastic goal long after my tormentors had thrown in the educational towel. It was their choice to leave at the first opportunity, but the really sad thing was that some of them were pretty bright and had begun their secondary education at a better grade than I had achieved.

Outside the classroom I continued with the sporting activities. Though still dreadfully lacking in confidence, I regularly represented the school at cricket and football, both at under-14s and later under-16s. The school had an excellent reputation at both, and being a part of that success certainly enhanced my approval rating with the staff.

But if I enjoyed a modicum of success with the school football and cricket teams, other aspects of physical education proved rather more challenging. Gymnastics was anathema and I steered clear of anything to do with vaulting, climbing or hanging upside down, no matter how momentarily.

Similarly problematical was country dancing, often employed as a fall back on days when poor weather prevented outside sporting activities. Picture this if you will: twenty disenchanted, spotty lads required to dance against their will and thus relate in some tactile way with twenty disinterested girls. All the participants wished they were a million miles away in a place not blessed with the dubious pleasures of the Gay Gordons or the Roger de Coverley – or was it Roger the Gay Gordons?

When country dancing was ramped up to ballroom dancing, the pain became a whole lot more excruciating. Waltzing consisted of twenty lads walking in a strangely crab-like manner and twenty girls walking in a similarly strange fashion in reverse, usually until a wall of the gym or another robotic couple impeded their progress. The inevitable tension that came with this level of visual contact between the sexes was further heightened by the preliminaries which required the boys to select a partner. The repercussions of an inappropriate choice amongst a class of tribal adolescents could have damaging implications that might come back to haunt you for some time to come.

I ploughed slowly on, unbowed by peer pressure, my acute lack of confidence and ballroom-dancing-induced embarrassment, until the prospect of GCEs loomed large on the horizon. My future life, or at least the one in my mind's eye, was beginning to take shape and I had a pretty good idea of what I needed to achieve. Now I just had to do it!

07

THE LION AWAKES

IT is no great surprise that we baby boomers looked across the Atlantic for our entertainment. Europe was on our doorstep, but back in the early sixties I felt no affinity with our near neighbours. Coca Cola, American movies and rock and roll seemed a whole lot more engaging than a continent still bowed by the aftermath of conflict – and, apart from anything else, there was the language problem. As I mentioned earlier, £50 package holidays to the Med were still some way off, and it wasn't until the mid-sixties that any trace of our continental friends gained recognition within the Elm household. That was via a bottle of Anjou Rosé, consumed reverently with our Christmas dinner!

Post-war Britain was struggling to find a new cultural identity, though there was a desire to rid it of the conservative attitudes that had roots as far back as Queen Victoria. The 1951 Festival of Britain demonstrated this will in terms of architecture and lifestyle, but it was no more than a pipe dream. The nation's economy was still in the doldrums. For popular culture, we boomers embraced the USA, its wealth of natural resources having facilitated a more rapid recovery to its post-wartime economy. This gave it a vitality that was missing in the UK, where we could still see evidence of the war.

With Elvis Presley and his cohort dominating the music charts, Cary Grant, Tony Curtis and the very beautiful Marilyn Monroe lighting up our silver screens, and with John F. Kennedy ensconced in the

White House, the USA appeared to have cornered the market in both showbiz and political glamour. All this would soon change, sadly and dramatically, aided and abetted by the nation's seemingly pathological hatred of anything vaguely socialist (communist), racial disquiet and an assassin's bullet.

It seemed to begin in 1961 with an abortive invasion of Cuba, where leader Fidel Castro was perceived to be cosying up to the USSR. Within a year, the Russian leader Nikita Khrushchev had done a deal with the Cuban government that potentially would result in Soviet missiles being deployed on the island only ninety miles from the American coast. For a while nuclear conflict seemed a real possibility. Happily, the powers-that-be managed to downgrade the situation by adding a few degrees of frost to the already chilly 'cold war'.

That particular crisis may have been averted but further disasters were just around the corner. The shocking assassination of JFK in 1963 was the overture to a litany of troubles that saw the US plunged into racial disharmony at home and all-out military conflict in Vietnam. It was a sad and sobering period in the nation's history and one that would tarnish its name. This was reflected upon by a new breed of songwriters, most notably Pete Seeger, Joan Baez and Bob Dylan, who used their medium to make their protest.

In marked contrast, the UK was starting to enjoy a feeling of change for the better. For me it started in 1962, when The Beatles debut single 'Love Me Do' crept into the UK top twenty (peaking at seventeen). It is a modest song involving a vocabulary of only eighteen words, composed of just one verse sung four times with a bridge between the second and third. The narrative is disturbingly simplistic, naive even; 'Bohemian Rhapsody' it most certainly is not.

From the perspective of a twelve-year-old kid, the words were pretty much superfluous; in any case I was hardly the Romeo of form 2B. No, forget the words: it was the song's musicality that appealed, a combination of pain, blues (though I had no idea what they were at the time), a soulful harmonica and a plodding rhythm that would have excited a Morris dancer. It was brilliant – and totally different to the

Yank crooners, their UK imitators and the twangy guitar groups that had dominated the music scene for some years.

As I said, it was a million miles from 'Bohemian Rhapsody' but I believe that we would not have had one without the other, and for us baby boomers it proved a pivotal moment.

As far as I was concerned, The Beatles might as well have fallen from space but, unbeknown to the vast majority of us, they had been honing their skills in clubs as far apart as Liverpool and Hamburg before suddenly exploding on the British music scene.

Equally significant was the avalanche of talent that followed in their wake, opening the door for a plethora of new bands and singer/ songwriters. The age of the guitar/vocal group had dawned, emanating from the cities of Liverpool and Manchester where new bands emerged with astonishing regularity. American acts, which had for so long enjoyed, unchallenged popularity at home in the US as well as in the UK, suddenly found themselves second billing to British groups on both sides of the Atlantic. Pop culture was upon us and destined to impact on the lives of a generation.

Its birth was not entirely pain free on account of it being disputed by highly adversarial twins. On one side were the so-called Rockers, who favoured leather jackets, greasy motor bikes and greasy hair, and whose musical proclivity tended to be backward looking toward rock 'n' roll. On the other side were Mods, who were influenced by Pop Art, preferred more progressive music, tailored suits, khaki-coloured parka coats and nothing more powerful than a scooter such as a Lambretta or Vespa. Cultural differences, yes, but surely not reasons to kick the crap out of one another. Nevertheless, going handbags at two paces is exactly what they did during the summer of 1964 on the beaches of Clacton and several towns along the south coast, much to the displeasure of the good citizens living there and Mr Plod the policeman.

Having overcome its birth pains, a new determination and optimism arose that defied all that had gone before. There was no way even a shrinking violet such as myself could avoid being caught up in the fervour for self-expression. In no time at all the youthful invasion had rejuvenated fashion and was about to transform popular music into something more significant and substantial.

The only thing holding back this second revolution was the media, who seemed ambivalent about it. For some time we were forced to feed our addiction by exploring the airwaves; many were the times my brother and I tuned our tiny transistor radio into the distant sounds of Radio Luxembourg, whose nightly broadcasts were just about the only access we had to all-out pop music. We did it despite the station being notoriously unpredictable and having a tendency to fade away, usually just as your favourite song came on!

Whilst Auntie Beeb continued to sit on her hands, persisting with archaic request programmes such as *Housewives' Choice* and *Two-way Family Favourites*, she left the door open for something to fill the void. We really didn't want to hear Max Bygraves singing 'Tulips From Amsterdam' as requested by Mrs Smith of 27 Sebastopol Terrace. Hell, no! We wanted The Who and Roger Daltry screaming 'bout 'My Generation'.

Something to fill the gap came in the form of 'pirate' radio stations, notably Radio Caroline and Radio London. Both were established in 1964 and could circumvent the BBC's monopoly by operating from vessels moored outside British territorial waters. They did so successfully until 1967, when the government passed a bill to outlaw unlicensed off-shore broadcasting.

It was not only popular culture that was changing; the winds of change were also blowing through the corridors of Parliament. In the October general election of 1964 the Labour Party, led by Harold Wilson, came to power and ended thirteen years of Tory rule. Their manifesto message was a simple one: to modernise Britain. Given the thirst for change and the desire to look forward rather than back, it was no great surprise when they won. The outgoing Tory government looked jaded and represented the past at a time when, understandably, the population wanted to look to the future.

At fourteen, like most kids of that age, I had other things to think about such as The Beatles' next record, acne and all manner of personal, adolescent, hang-ups. There is, after all, nothing more irritating than a politically motivated teenager, as demonstrated by sixteen-year-old William Hague making his sycophantic speech to the Tory Party Conference in 1977. Google it, but make sure you have a sick bag handy!

Post-war austerity was receding at last. With the improving economic climate came an expansive programme of building projects for libraries, hospitals, schools and infrastructure. The M1 was extending northward from London, and even my school at Hatfield was eventually completed, albeit about a year late. Its distinctive construction of exposed Meccano-like steel beams and its skin of glass, concrete and coloured metal panels, became the architectural language of the sixties.

During this period of rebuilding, successive governments set about the difficult task of redistributing the nation's wealth in order to deliver a fairer, more just society. In 1966 Ray Davies, front man for The Kinks, wrote two songs that reflected the polarised opposites within the nation: 'Dead End Street', a graphic description of the hopelessness of bedsit land, and 'Sunny Afternoon', written from the perspective of the landed gentry bemoaning the threats to their privileged lifestyle. Each is a masterpiece, both in terms of musical wit and social history.

An economic renaissance was underway, bringing optimism and a cultural revolution. The 'swinging sixties' were here with their unstoppable musical diversification and dynamic new fashion culture that was epitomised by Mary Quant, Twiggy and Carnaby Street. Britain had finally shaken off post-war austerity and was flexing more positive and prosperous muscles reflected in a wave of patriotism expressed in the slogan 'I'm Backing Britain'.

For me 'Ob-La-Di, Ob-La-Da', another Beatles' song from 1968, captures the optimism of this time. Above all, it is a happy song indicative of a country in a better frame of mind and more at one with itself. It is a celebration of normality and contentment. Furthermore, the use of a ska-music rhythm, hardly ever heard before in the UK, hints at a more multi-cultural society.

08

1966 : THE GOOD, THE BAD AND THE UGLY

BEFORE you go jumping to the wrong conclusion, this section of my scrapbook is not about a low-budget spaghetti western though, by coincidence, it does share the same date. Instead it is a reflection of three things that occurred during those twelve months, all of which had a significant impact on the nation, particularly on those people directly and indirectly affected by them.

The Good

After years of waiting, the World Cup had arrived! Strangely enough, the nation did not appear to be overly excited by the prospect; there seemed to be low expectations of a national team that hadn't, it has to be said, been particularly successful in recent years.

As hosts, England had the honour of starting the proceedings and played out a dismal goalless draw with Uruguay. It seemed the doubters might be right after all. In Mexico they found less resolute opposition and won 2–0, so on the evening of the 20th of July they faced France in the last of the group qualifying rounds. Victory would mean certain qualification as group leaders.

I remember the evening very well as it coincided with my school's open event at which I, along with a number of classmates, were to present a demonstration on behalf of the science department. During the course of our lessons we had been making a large tissue-paper balloon in readiness for the demo beneath which, come the hour, we would create a heat source by way of a naked flame. So no fire hazard there then! And lo! Members of the fifth form did make the balloon rise and fall in the stairwell of B Block without needing the fire brigade! I can't even begin to think how many health and safety rules and fire regulations this would contravene today.

Throughout the evening there was a constant buzz as information was passed amongst pupils, teachers and parents about the latest score from Wembley. Eventually the news came through that England had won 2–0. (Oh, and, yeah, yeah, we get it – hot air rises!) Sure enough, England were through to the quarter finals where they would meet very stiff opposition in the form of Argentina.

The quarter final was a turbulent, tetchy affair. Even with a man sent off, Argentina made it very difficult but were eventually overcome by a single goal. By now there seemed to be new belief. Even the brilliance of Eusebio in the semi-final could not prevent England from prevailing over a talented Portuguese team that happily returned to playing the game rather than engaging in warfare, a tactic they had employed to destroy the talented Brazilians.

The scene was set for a final against the old enemy, West Germany. It was a confrontation hyped by national pride and more than a little prejudice. Surely we wouldn't lose in England's green and pleasant land to the Germans? *Anyone* but the Germans!

I need tell you nothing about the match; it has been documented many times by authors more qualified than me. Suffice to say that I, along with the rest of the country, was feeling pretty chipper with England leading 2–1 only seconds before the final whistle. But you can never write off those plucky Germans and, after a goal-mouth skirmish not dissimilar in its chaotic appearance to Poussin's painting *Rape of the Sabine Women*, they contrived an equalizer with virtually the last kick of the ninety minutes.

I'm ashamed to admit it, but this was all too much for me. I remember going out into my parents' garden, unable to watch as the game went into extra time. As I paced around, I became aware of a strange and eerie silence that had descended over the neighbourhood. It seemed the nation's population were sitting transfixed by what they were watching on their TV screens.

Eventually the silence was broken by a cheer that sounded along the street and quite possibly the length and breadth of the land. I raced into the house expecting to see the team celebrating, but instead saw a huddle of German players remonstrating with the linesman and referee. Had the ball crossed the line or not?

It's difficult to imagine what kind of deliberation could have transpired between a Swiss referee and an Azerbaijani linesman, but the outcome was that, rightly or wrongly, the referee signalled a goal and the nation breathed again. To their great credit the Germans never gave up, and the following minutes of the match seemed an eternity. Then came that magic moment, that totally wonderful moment when a last-gasp German attack broke down and the ball was hoofed down the pitch.

Whistle in mouth, the referee was looking at his watch, an action that prompted a few spectators to run on the pitch thinking the match had ended. Fortunately Geoff Hurst was oblivious to this commotion; he summoned up one final burst of energy to run on and smash the ball past the hapless goalkeeper into the roof of the net.

Kenneth Wolstenholme's brilliantly spontaneous commentary is now legendary. '*Some people are on the pitch,*' he said, '*…they think it's all over … it is now.*' It still gives me goose bumps every time I see it.

The 1966 England squad played as a team proud to wear their nation's jersey and with only a modest reward for their endeavours. Geoff Hurst's published account of the time leading up to and beyond the final informs us that all twenty-two members of the England squad received bonuses of £1,000 pounds. Not exactly a king's ransom, even allowing for inflation.

On the day after the final, he and his wife Judith took a taxi back to their semi-detached house in Hornchurch, Essex, where he proceeded to mow the lawn and wash his car. I'm not prone to use the word 'hero' when it comes to describing sports personalities, or anyone other than those who put their lives at risk for others, but I think these guys and their coach, Alf Ramsey, fully deserved the honours bestowed upon them.

The Bad

This was the icing on the cake. The nation was on top of its game, enjoying an economic renaissance, and now we held the World Cup for the first time in our history. It truly was a memorable time for the country, and for me. But as we basked in this national glory, an incident occurred that was as abhorrent as winning the World Cup was a triumph, and it seemed to cast a sombre shadow over all that had gone before.

On the 12th of August, barely two weeks after the final, three policemen were shot dead by an armed robber called Harry Roberts. Perhaps such things had happened before but I thought that police officers were somehow guarded by unwritten laws that provided them with a sort of physical and moral protection. Surely this kind of thing only happened on the streets of New York and in American gangster movies?

This sad episode seems to have been a watershed moment for all the worst reasons. Since then, death and violence on the streets have hardened society to this sort of appalling crime. As a result, life appears to have become cheap, something that is substantiated by government statistics. In 1966 there were 364 recorded murders in England and Wales, but by the millennium this had risen to 850. Similarly worrying is the alarming increase in violent crime, which rose from 52,498 recorded cases to 741,954, a percentage increase that cannot be justified by the comparatively small increase in population.

I find these highly disturbing statistics and I am angered when I hear subsequent generations trying to downplay them, frequently with a dismissive counterclaim that my generation looks back at its early decades through rose-tinted spectacles. That being the case, it is becoming difficult to remain positive about our future.

In earlier chapters I described my formative years. For many of us they were simple times with modest expectations and little luxury, but above all else they were stable and within a society that recognised a code that generally worked well. It wasn't perfect and, yes, there was crime, but it was a million miles from where we are today. Expectation has grown out of all proportion, which inevitably leads to discontent and very possibly a whole lot worse.

The UK of the fifties and sixties was by no means utopian; there was much to do in order to improve society. However, I would argue that it was a more stable place in the summer of 1966 than at any time since.

The Ugly

Later that same year, there was another catastrophe. On the 21st of October, a school in Aberfan, Wales, was enveloped by more than a hundred cubic metres of slag from the adjoining colliery, causing the death of 116 children and twenty-eight adults. It was reported that the National Coal Board had illegally tipped the slag onto land containing water springs and a prolonged period of rain had caused the debris to become unstable.

As a result of a tribunal report in 1969, new legislation was passed to remedy the apparent absence of regulations in connection with mining and quarry spoil, which makes you wonder how such a disaster had never happened before.

We had stopped sending kids into mines and up chimneys with brushes and all manner of other industrial mayhem, thanks largely to the inception of the trade unions and a number of influential, philanthropic industrialists. However, our industrial base was seriously under-regulated until the Health and Safety at Work Act of 1974 and the subsequent founding of the Health and Safety Executive. Only then was workplace health, safety and welfare regulated with powers of enforcement and legal sanctions.

⊙⊙⊙

The murder of the policemen was a warning to our social and moral standing; the tragedy at Aberfan reminded us that we needed to be more vigilant in our everyday working lives and the practices that govern them. My research suggests that we have not heeded the warning signs of the former but have been significantly more proactive in the latter. Unfortunately, the more recent performances of our national football team speak for themselves. As I write, some fifty years on from that memorable day at Wembley, the nation's long wait for similar success shows little sign of ending.

09

THE CHOSEN ONES AND
THE BEAUTIFUL PEOPLE

BY the mid-sixties, racial disharmony, social injustice and clashes of ideology had given rise to much disquiet throughout the western world. In the UK 'I'm Backing Britain' flags gave way to Campaign for Nuclear Disarmament (CND) logos as the mood changed from one of national optimism to that of international outrage on account of the USA's continuing intervention in Vietnam.

This was a mere shadow of what was happening in the USA itself. Here was a nation troubled not only by the human and economic misery of war but also by racial tension, both being challenged by way of mass rallies and often violent demonstrations. The exuberance of the American dream was losing its gloss. In musical terms, the clean-cut, all-American innocence of its mainstream pop icons was starting to be eclipsed by songs of dissent and protest.

I have already mentioned Dylan, Baez and Seeger, all of whom continued their crusades, but their message was now being echoed by many more. Songs like Country Joe McDonald's 'Feels-Like-I'm-Fixing-To-Die Rag', Barry McGuire's 'Eve Of Destruction' and John Lennon's 'Give Peace A Chance' made powerful statements and struck a chord with the ever-growing army of anti-war campaigners.

Interestingly, in many respects Don McLean's 1971 song, 'American

Pie', is an allegorical reflection on this time, though the imagery he employs to convey his thoughts is challenging, to say the least. Many have attempted to interpret his linguistic gymnastics but I feel safer placing my trust in the man himself. Nearly forty-five years later he decided to sell his song notes and, for the first time, provided some explanation.

Basically in 'American Pie' things are heading in the wrong direction. It (life) is becoming less idyllic. I don't know whether you consider that wrong or right, but it is a morality song in a sense.

There is little doubt that his starting point for the song was the death of Buddy Holly in 1959 with nostalgic references to the period. From then on, and through all manner of symbolism, he describes how cynicism replaced innocence within the music scene and across American society in general. He used the deaths of John F. Kennedy, Bobby Kennedy and civil rights leader Martin Luther King (whom he refers to as the Father, Son and Holy Ghost) as a metaphor for how American society was losing its way and falling into moral decline. Above all else, it is a song that describes a nation at odds with itself and at a crossroads socially, culturally and on the world stage.

This period gave rise to the formation of an anti-establishment counterculture that challenged the values of American society and opposed the war in Vietnam, whilst promoting spiritual and meditative practices and sexual freedom. The followers went in search of a more simple, less materialistic lifestyle and founded the 'Summer of Love'.

It is generally thought that this took root in the Haight-Ashbury District of San Francisco, and its message was forever enshrined in Scott McKenzie's classic song 'San Francisco (Be Sure To Wear Some Flowers In Your Hair)'. A new generation of Americans, together with their counterparts across the western world, had had enough of the troubles and war and indulged themselves by way of psychedelic, flower-powered, hippy-happy (and in many cases drug-fuelled) musical love-ins. And whilst the Summer of Love might not have radically altered American society, it proved a tangible moment in time that signalled a turning point in the history of popular music and heralded a golden decade. It was a landmark in rock history, a launchpad from which so much musical creativity emanated, and it also gave birth to the phenomenon of the music festival.

There would be many music festivals, notably Monterey and Woodstock in the USA, and the Isle of Wight and Glastonbury in the UK, the latter becoming the most celebrated and durable. Rob Young, in his expansive tome *Electric Eden: Unearthing Britain's Visionary Music*, described the 1971 Glastonbury Fayre (as it was then called) as a gathering that included a broad spectrum of folk from the religious to the pagan.

There was something beyond flower power at work: the momentary lifting of a veil that revealed a British society in a parallel universe; a fleeting social experiment and celebration that has never, despite numerous attempts, been repeated in quite the same way since.

By all accounts it was an orderly event, with no alcohol sold, only vegetarian food available and with instructions to:

break bread with strangers, share and conserve water and food, refrain from damaging local crops and to clap more quietly to respect residents' desire for peace.

However, this seemingly conservative mantra did not deter:

...spliffs being puffed and passed around ... Hare Krishna devotees chanting over tamburas ... pipe-puffing or denim-clad Anglican vicars joining throbbing circles of Jesus-haired dancers ... and decidedly un-English nudity.

I'd dearly love to have been at any of these events. Even an introvert like me couldn't have failed to score in that sort of environment, though my reluctance to dance around bollock naked in public (I don't like dancing), and my aversion to sticking anything in my mouth that is burning at the other end may have curbed my exuberance. Come to think of it, who am I kidding? I'd never have survived.

Some thirty years later I eventually made it to Glastonbury, but not before it had been appropriated by a post-Thatcherite generation whose legions seemed more intent on hugging their cell phones than anyone in their midst. Gone were the naked, flower-adorned dancers, the drug culture, the ne'er-do-wells and the gatecrashers; in had come law and order, catering and a huge perimeter security fence.

The old romantic in me hated the changes but, being the person I am, I welcomed the mundane normality of it all. I guess I'm just not cut out for bohemia, much as I might like to think I am. I had to face up to the fact that, though I might have been a child of the fifties and sixties, flower power and all that, I was now an old git of the new millennium with a mortgage, a family, an accountant and a fondness for privy privacy, something that is in short supply at Glastonbury.

⊙⊙⊙

By this time the music scene was becoming a very significant part of my life and the lives of pretty much the entire generation of baby boomers, whether by way of social comment, expression of love or protest. This passion for music was reflected in sales, where the LP began to replace the single as the industry's currency, and where The Beatles continued to lead the way in terms of musical innovation. On a recent CD issue of The Moody Blues seminal album of 1966, *Days Of Future Passed*, which I recently acquired to replace my vinyl copy (swapped in a brief moment of insanity), music writer Mark Powell, includes in his sleeve notes:

The exceptional achievements and musical shift of The Beatles did not go unnoticed within the British music industry, with many other artists now eager to push the boundaries of popular music into territory previously uncharted. Artists with a background in Rhythm and Blues and Beat music soon began to undergo a rapid stylistic change. The Moody Blues were no exception, and like The Beatles, their music would be a huge influence on a generation of musicians who would pioneer so-called 'progressive' rock.

At this time The Beatles famously announced they would never tour again, preferring to perform in the recording studio rather than at venues where thousands of screaming kids effectively blotted out their music. It was a decision that would see their work become more complex and sophisticated, notably in the *Sgt. Pepper's Lonely Hearts*

Club Band album, released in May 1967. In its wake there was a wealth of inventive albums from a hugely talented generation of singers and songwriters who exploited new technology and better instruments in pursuance of their craft.

As this rich vein of music progressed, it was championed by new radio programmes with enlightened presenters, most notably 'Whispering' Bob Harris and John Peel. They, like several of their colleagues, had been seduced from pirate radio stations by the BBC. The airwaves now echoed to the sounds of a huge variety of fresh talent.

In any edition of the *John Peel Show*, the one thing you could be sure of was that you couldn't be sure of anything. It was edgy and experimental, an eclectic amalgamation of all that was new, different, progressive and often weird. It was beyond mainstream pop music and it nurtured my new-found interest in folk music, which had been initiated by two albums: Fairport Convention's *What We Did On Our Holiday*, my bridge to what would become known as folk-rock, and *Bert And John* by Bert Jansch and John Renbourn, an album that led me to the band Pentangle and their unique mixture of folk-blues and traditional, plus the occasional excursion into medieval music. Both routes inevitably led me to Shirley Collins, the first lady of English traditional music.

Being an incurable romantic, I was immediately smitten by their modern interpretations of traditional folk songs. Porcelain-skinned Pre-Raphaelite girls being deflowered in medieval settings, or tales of seduction in England's green and pleasant land, were the perfect sustenance for my hungry imagination.

You don't have to dig too deeply to realise that many traditional folk songs about love and sex are completely and utterly non-PC. They are largely dependent on stereotypes where the women are fey, gullible innocents and the men are feckless bastards – preferably Irish feckless bastards. They are no more than tales of times long gone, both good and bad, and should be taken as such, nothing more. Simply add a rhythm section, an electric guitar and a sexy female voice to enjoy the full effect.

Soon afterwards, TV embraced musical diversification beyond that represented by programmes such as *Top of the Pops* and *Ready Steady Go!*. I recall a pivotal moment in 1969 when Jimi Hendrix, unlikely as it may seem now, was booked to play the BBC's light entertainment *Happening for Lulu* show. He clearly hadn't read the script requiring him to sing the end of 'Hey Joe' as a duet with Lulu. Who the hell thought that would work?

Having started with a rendition of 'Voodoo Child' that could have blown the froth off a cappuccino from fifty paces, he dutifully began playing 'Hey Joe' but stopped halfway through saying, '*We'd like to stop playing this rubbish and dedicate a song to Cream, regardless of what kind of group they may be in. We dedicate this to Eric Clapton, Ginger Baker and Jack Bruce.*' He and his band promptly launched into an instrumental version of Cream's 'Sunshine Of Your Love', hijacking the duet and over-running the live broadcast. The producer went apeshit, and Hendrix was banned by the BBC.

But the broadcasting companies could no longer ignore rock music. In 1971 the BBC, bless 'em, introduced T*he Old Grey Whistle Test*, the first TV show dedicated to contemporary musicians whose work was not geared to variety shows, discos or the hit parade. Alas, Jimi Hendrix would not live long enough to be a part of it.

A new approach to contemporary music was born and, even at an embryonic stage, was starting to stand alone. As we became more earnest in listening to music, we demanded better equipment on which to play it. I, for example, eventually blew a sizeable portion of my first pay packet on a new stereo system. This replaced two previous generations of record players, including the aforementioned Disc Jockey Junior, which had gone to pastures new (or the tip) some while earlier. Who would have thought that nearly fifty years later those anonymous little record players, with their asthmatic speakers, arthritic mechanism and grey complexion of textured Fablon, would make a comeback helped by self-appointed, millennial style gurus eager to misconstrue words like 'retro' and 'fashion' as a benchmark for quality? Well, there you are: I've said it now, and I suddenly feel a grumpy old man looking over my shoulder!

10

TECHNOLOGICAL REVOLUTION # 1
– MAN ON THE MOON

DURING my life I may have garnered some understanding and comprehension of world events, but the concept of technology (or the 'appliance of science', to appropriate an old Zanussi slogan) has often been lost on me.

The inventions featured in the BBC's *Tomorrow's World*, first broadcast in 1965, were all very well but never really excited me. Items such as the pocket calculator were ingenious but only on a domestic level; it seemed to me that nothing was really tearing up the life manual and saying, '*This is how it's going to be from now on.*'

Then, in June 1967, the BBC achieved its first ever trans-world TV satellite link-up, and in one fell swoop the world seemed to become a smaller place. The UK's contribution to this memorable event featured The Beatles singing 'All You Need Is Love', which at the time I perceived as a hippy, flower-power anthem. Subsequently I discovered that it was commissioned specially for the programme, its simple message designed to be accessible to the international audience receiving the broadcast.

No doubt it seemed to be the perfect message to deliver to the world, especially at a time when the Vietnam war was showing no sign of reaching a conclusion. What I didn't understand (and I don't think many of us did other than the boffins in white coats) was how this technological breakthrough was going to change the world forever. Within a generation we would all be able to hold private video links with people on the other side of the world from the comfort of our own homes.

Although the science behind worldwide broadcasting eluded me, the tangible reality of Concorde's maiden flight, on the 2nd of March 1969 most certainly did not. It seemed to be one of those pivotal moments when you felt technology had leapt forward by fifty years in the space of an hour. The evidence was there before us in a futuristic form that seemed far more compelling than the slightly dodgy black-and-white TV pictures produced by the satellite broadcast. The prospect of flying from London to New York more quickly than the train could travel from London to Edinburgh was astonishing, even if such a prospect was unlikely to come my way.

The aircraft had its doubters and critics but, no matter what you thought of Concorde, you have to admit she was an astonishingly beautiful aircraft. The other rather nice aspect of this Anglo-French project was that, for once, we had achieved something ahead of the Americans and the Russians. Both countries had similar aspirations but spat out their dummies when they realised they were losing this particular technological race.

However, a few months later the Americans would go, as only they can, not one but a thousand technological steps further when Neil Armstrong stepped on the surface of the moon. The Russians had put a satellite into space in 1957 and a man into orbit in 1961, acts that the USA perceived as threatening to their national security (or was it just their pride?). Their response was swift: a month after Yuri Gagarin became the first Russian cosmonaut, President Kennedy announced that the USA intended to have a man on the moon before the end of the decade. On the 20th of July 1969, they achieved just that.

Confirmation of a safe lunar landing came through in the early hours, and I recall waiting bleary-eyed to see it. Eventually a faint picture flickered onto our TV of the quality not unlike those coaxed from our first set back in the fifties by my father's desperate trial-and-error tuning. The difference now was that these faint, almost ghostly images were travelling nearly 240,000 miles from the surface of the moon to Australia and then bouncing 12,000 miles around the world to us. At that point the significance of those poor-quality images of the first satellite broadcast a couple of years earlier became clear to me.

As these first pictures of the lunar landscape flashed to all corners of the globe, much of the world's population looked on in disbelief at what they were seeing. I was no exception; to this day, I feel privileged to have witnessed this momentous event. I will never forget seeing Neil Armstrong step down onto the moon's surface and utter the words, '*One small step for man, one giant leap for mankind*'.

For one wonderful and all too brief moment in time, there seemed to be a spirit of unity around the world in celebration of human endeavour. And who can ever forget those stunning pictures of the earth rising above the lunar horizon – they were literally out of this world. We saw ourselves as never before. If recent scientific achievements had seemed to shrink our world, this one brought home the fact that we were a tiny part of the cosmos, little more than a speck of dust in an eternity of endless space.

This achievement happened at a time when computer technology was more akin to the wartime bombe machine operated by my mother and the Bletchley code breakers than anything we have today. Those that made it possible were dependent on slide rules and the like for their most crucial calculations. Since then, we have progressed rapidly from punchcard technology to microchips, and from huge cabinets with winding spools that assimilated relatively small amounts of information to computers about the size of a chocolate bar that can connect you to the world via phone and the internet. And they can take photographs and do a million and one other things, 999,995 of which we don't really need. Or, maybe, I just missed too many episodes of *Tomorrow's World*!

Unfortunately, while the USA was pursuing its quest to become the rulers of space, it rather overlooked its own housekeeping, an oversight that would eventually impact on the space programme. NASA's budget for delivering man to the moon was astronomical. By the end of the decade the economics of the project were being questioned by the national press who, until then, had been filling column inches with space-travel rhetoric. There was much cynicism in the poorer sections of society, not least the black population, who found themselves at the rump end of a socio-economic dilemma. This predicament drove pioneer rap artist Gil Scott-Heron to write 'Whitey On The Moon', a poem (and later a song) that expressed the growing disquiet. In seeking space supremacy, and in response to Russian competition, the USA had been washed along on a wave of euphoria without considering the true cost and who was paying it.

Since then, space exploration has become rather more pragmatic; at least, that is how it appears to a non-techie like me. That's not to say it has been without its highs (and sadly some desperate lows). The International Space Station is a multi-national exercise, an amazing achievement that facilitates a range of scientific research. Linked to this, the Americans developed the shuttle, the first craft capable of flying back into the Earth's atmosphere and therefore being reusable and fundamental to construction of the space station.

It was the shuttle that featured in two of the space industry's worst disasters. The first happened on the 28th of January 1986, when the shuttle Challenger and its launch rocket exploded within minutes of lifting off, killing all seven crew members. I recall the moment vividly and the feeling of total disbelief. Being televised in a live broadcast, it reminded me of an incident some nineteen years earlier when Donald Campbell lost his life trying to break the water-speed record on Lake Coniston. Sadly, the shuttle Columbia suffered a similar fate in February 2003, this time exploding whilst re-entering the earth's atmosphere.

More positively, there have been some spectacularly successful unmanned exploratory missions to Mars and beyond that have sent back pictures and data I never thought to see in my lifetime. Unlike my eighteen-year-old self, the one unmoved by anything scientific, I am continually amazed by man's ingenuity in pushing back boundaries that seemed impenetrable not so long ago.

11

'WHAT YOU NEED IS A GOOD BAD WOMAN'

I'D like to say that I entered my arty-farty phase as my secondary education came to a close, but that was never going to happen. I was a painfully introverted, self-conscious guy from a council estate, destined to become a half-decent draughtsman but never an artist. I didn't have the imagination for all that stuff, and I didn't have an ego big enough to want to cut cows in half and claim they were art, or look at my wrecked bed and think, '*Wow... a masterpiece! I'll just give Mr Saatchi a ring.*'

Don't get me wrong; I admire creativity and innovation in the arts very much. It just seems to me that much of what is passed off today under the spurious banner of 'modern' or 'fine' art amounts to little more than elitist, quasi-intellectual snobbery that boosts the egos of its creators and panders to a small, cultish following of wealthy socialite patrons. A close friend of mine often refers to them as the 'Billy Bonkers Society', which I find apt. In that context, the expression 'the king's new clothes' also springs to mind.

I finished my secondary school days pretty much as shy and self-conscious as the day I started them. I was resigned to the fact I would never enjoy the company of the beautiful Margaret from the lower sixth, whom I had admired for some time but never had the bottle to approach. Academically, however, I had been rather more successful, gaining a respectable clutch of O levels and a couple of A levels, as well as being a house captain and head boy. Not too bad for an eleven-plus reject.

I was lucky to be at the right school at the right time, where a fresh new staff were as keen to prove themselves as I was to learn. I shall always be indebted to them for their enthusiasm and 'can do' attitude.

Despite my obvious failings, I considered myself pretty fortunate. I had navigated school exams and, unlike many of my contemporaries, I knew exactly what career I wanted to follow. I had cultivated an interest in gardening (sorry about the pun) and the wider environment and had a little artistic ability, so the idea of becoming a landscape architect seemed logical. My only problem now was finding the confidence to achieve this. Most people would have applied to college and gained a professional qualification, but I wasn't ready for that. Instead I decided to put college on a back burner as a longer-term ambition and started looking for work.

No employment opportunities came along until the autumn, when I secured a job with the East Herts Divisional Planning Office based in Hertford. It didn't put me in a design environment but it was in a profession allied to landscape. It also offered some useful experience, though to be honest *any* office experience was going to be valuable to someone as green as myself.

I had two main duties. The first was completing land-search forms, the mechanism by which solicitors garner planning information that may affect land or property, usually when the ownership is being conveyed from one party to another. It was fairly important work but deadly boring. The second rather more interesting task was assisting planning officers by providing them with the background history to any site for which they had received a new application. For my efforts,

I received the princely sum of £600.00 per annum.

Life in an office was a whole new ballgame, not least because I was now actually required to speak to women. Not surprisingly, my difficulties with this gave rise to a certain amount of good-humoured mirth, particularly when I was drawn into conversation with the office junior who had legs up to her armpits and breasts like the bow of an aircraft carrier. She was sixteen going on twenty-nine, and I was eighteen going on clueless!

Derek, with whom I shared duties, was particularly amused by my shortcomings. He was five or six years my senior, though it felt like a generation of difference such was his confidence at work. He used to say to me, 'W*hat you need, Oswald,*' – I never found out why he occasionally called me Oswald – '*is a good bad woman.*' Maybe he was right.

Social shortcomings apart, I had a good start to my working life. After a couple of years, a new opportunity came my way as if part of the perfect career course. I was sitting in the office one day, ploughing through my allocation of searches and applications, when one of the planning officers called me over. He introduced me to a man called Gordon Patterson, a well-respected landscape architect who had his own practice and was a consultant to Stevenage Development Corporation. We had a brief conversation. He mentioned a position that was about to be advertised at the corporation and said he would forward the job description as soon as it was available.

Within a few weeks I had been interviewed and taken the job of landscape tracer – for which I would enjoy a pay rise of £235.00.

I took to the new job at Stevenage like a duck to water. The work was interesting and I had a whole new typing pool to fantasise about. I remember that on my very first day one of the senior typists strolled into our office and said, '*I've come to see the new talent!*'

Despite my continued lack of success with women, I was starting to find my direction in life. I was being paid to draw and be creative in a team that had invaluable experience and knowledge. I was surrounded by people who understood the environment and I was working in a more relaxed office where the emphasis was on design. This lent itself to a more laid-back dress code that I was happy to exploit, notably with a combination of crimson crew-necked sweater and flared crimson cord trousers. I must have looked like a Goth's glow stick!

Though I had chosen not to go to college, I was starting to feel the need for my own space. At that time the corporation had a reasonable turnover of rented accommodation, so it wasn't long before I was assembling a few basic bits of furniture and striking out on a wholly new experience.

I was merely putting off the inevitable, however, and soon found myself at a crossroads. I enjoyed three years with the corporation but my career had stalled. Without the necessary professional qualification, I could not progress at Stevenage – or anywhere else for that matter.

The following year I gained a place at Leeds Polytechnic. I took advantage of a scheme where the corporation sponsored employees through their professional training if they returned to work during vacations and committed to two years' post-qualification service. I had a few concerns about signing up for six years but, having given it some thought, I decided I was not prepared to risk the job market four years hence and opted in. As it turned out, the whole thing would become academic...

12

HALCYON DAYS

THE decision to go to college brought to an end five carefree years during which I'd gained a lot of useful work experience but otherwise had free wheeled.

It was a time when London was the place to be and new trends in music, fashion and style were constantly evolving. Notice my use of the words 'constantly evolving' rather than commercially imposed; the difference was that a generation was liberating itself from decades of stagnation rather than becoming slaves to commercialism.

To soak up some of the scene (as we used to say), I occasionally went to London with my pal Ian (the one whose junior-school football prowess made Maradona look a bit of a slouch) to trawl the record stores in Oxford Street and Tottenham Court Road, or visit the Carnaby Street boutiques, the centre of all that was 'fab' in town.

Richard Branson had just opened his first Virgin record shop in rather unlikely premises above a drab shoe shop, though the huge rainbow pattern on its first-floor frontage did distinguish it from its mundane neighbour. Once you'd negotiated the stairs up to the store, you entered a gloomy space where hairy rock dudes thumbed record racks or took the sounds on earphones whilst perched on beanbags. It was the place to be, man!

There was an ulterior motive to our forays into London: it gave us an opportunity to survey the trendy city girls. Mini-skirts were in, bras were out; there were plenty of pretty young things, uninhibited and unabashed, happy to be out in cool May breeze. And why not? It put colour into the cheeks and a spring in the step of many a young man. Well, it worked for me!

The music scene continued to blossom. Those doyens of folk rock, Fairport Convention and Pentangle, now had to share my attention with more diverse sounds. It all started when a friend played me the album *Led Zeppelin II*. I had been so preoccupied, living in the musical past, that I was blinkered to much of what was going on around me. I had some catching up to do.

It was the start of a journey that took me back in time before going forward. I needed to take another look at the impact of The Beatles and some of the other bands that had made waves during the mid to late sixties, and the phenomenon that is often referred to as the 'Brit Invasion' of the USA. It is well documented that its impact pretty much ended the era of doo-wop crooners and hastened the demise of Motown and the 'surf's-up' beach-bum brigade. But how did this happen? How could white bands, inspired by blues roots music, succeed in America?

In many respects it was a case of self-destruction, the seeds of which were sown in the USA itself. By the mid-fifties, blues music was becoming very unpopular even within the black American community, and swing music (something enjoyed multilaterally) was giving way to rockabilly and rock 'n' roll, which further disenfranchised blues musicians. As a result, many could barely scrape a living.

It wasn't until several of them made European tours that their fortunes changed. In the UK they found willing and eager disciples amongst fledgling Brit bands such as The Animals, The Yardbirds, The Rolling Stones, Fleetwood Mac and John Mayall's Blues Breakers. Here the name Bert Jansch crops up again; he was particularly influential during this period. At the time of Jansch's death, Jimmy Page of Led Zeppelin described him as, *'the innovator of the time ... so far ahead of what anyone else was doing.'*

Like me, these musicians had been looking to the past for inspiration, but where I'd been travelling metaphorically down country lanes seeking out Morris dancers on verdant village greens, they had been delving into the smoky clubs and backstreets of Chicago, Detroit and New Orleans via the back streets of London.

Very soon their live performances were underpinned by the work of bluesmen Big Bill Broonzy, B.B. King, Elmore James, Muddy Waters and – perhaps the most celebrated of them all – Robert Johnson.

Eric Clapton wrote in the sleeve notes to his 2004 album *Me and Mr Johnson*:

It is a remarkable thing ... to have been driven and influenced all of my life by the work of one man. And even though I accept that it has always been the keystone of my musical foundation, I still would not regard it as an obsession, instead I prefer to think of it as a landmark that I navigate by, whenever I feel myself going adrift.

British musicians had taken American blues music and reinvented it. In so doing, they made it more palatable to both the black and white populations of the USA.

If you want an example, try listening to Led Zeppelin's 'Since I've Been Loving You' from their third album released in 1970. Written by Robert Plant, Jimmy Page and John Paul Jones, it is a classic piece of blues, and I'm sure any of the bluesmen I've mentioned would have been more than happy to call it their own.

This trend inevitably prompted a resurgence of interest in blues music, something reflected upon by Colin Escott in his sleeve notes for the album B.B. King *His Definitive Greatest Hits*.

During 1969, B.B. played to more people than during all other years of his career combined. The following year, he became the first bluesman to appear on the Tonight Show, and then, in October 1970, over 70 million people saw him on the Ed Sullivan Show. The blues had arrived on prime time; it had only taken 50 years.

The renaissance, now in full flow, saw a plethora of American musicians become empowered to embrace black Afro-American influences that had been suppressed by generations of cultural and musical racism. Their new music was inspired not only by the blues but also by soul, country, jazz and Latin sounds. Steely Dan, Little Feat, The Doobie Brothers, Chicago, The Eagles, Santana, Bonnie Raitt and Linda Ronstadt all now figured in my burgeoning record collection. It makes me wonder what Elvis Presley might have morphed into had his early career not been set against the backdrop of a racially-divided society and had he not been seduced by the spangled jumpsuit.

I don't want to go into too much navel gazing about the term 'rock music' because, if I'm not very careful, I'll find myself using words like 'fusion' and 'idiom', and spouting all manner of pretentious crap. Nevertheless, it was an auspicious time in the annals of twentieth-century music.

I can only mention a few of the bands and musicians who brought about this musical phenomenon, but I must make some attempt to illustrate the range of music that was evolving in the first few years of the seventies.

At the more commercial end there was someone who lived just a few miles from my home town. He was a nerdy-looking little bloke called Reg Dwight, whose only claim to fame as far as I could see was being the nephew of Roy Dwight, a star of the 1958 Cup Final and one of my fifteen-quid-a-week football legends. Somewhere along the line from pub pianist to the release of his first record, Reg's name had changed to Elton John. By the time I was fortunate enough to see him at the less than salubrious Hemel Hempstead Pavilion, his star was very much in the ascendant. He was good – very, very good – but I don't think for one moment that the audience imagined he'd later fill Madison Square Garden in New York and make regular appearances in Las Vegas.

You could say that Elton John and Bernie Taupin's music transcended pop and rock in that they combined commercial songs aimed at the music mainstream with more diverse music where blues, country, soul and gospel influences lurked just beneath the surface – but that is getting perilously close to pretentious geek speak. What you can say about him is that he gave a huge amount of pleasure during the 1970s to a wide variety of people and continues to do so to this day.

In 1973, something completely different arrived that made me and all devotees of mid-Atlantic, bell-bottomed, Fender-guitared rock music think again. Mike Oldfield stepped forward and proceeded to mess with all our heads with *Tubular Bells*, a piece of contemporary music in classical format consisting of a single composite work. Yes, there had been concept albums where songs and music attempted to portray a common theme, but nothing like this. Instrumentals in any shape or form had been pretty unfashionable for some time; the last one I'd bought was three minutes and fifteen seconds of 'Telstar' by the Tornados back in 1962. An almost entirely instrumental album was unusual and some thought misguided, but the doubters were proved wrong. I would suggest it was as much a seminal moment of twentieth-century music as The Beatles *Sgt. Pepper*.

Arguably *Tubular Bells* did less for its creator than it did for the man who saw, or rather heard, its potential and set up a record company to release it. Richard Branson's new Virgin record label expand from retail record sales to include a recording company, all of which he eventually sold to EMI in 1995 for a cool five hundred million pounds.

Branson gave support and opportunity to many musicians who otherwise might not have seen the light of day. It was that sort of patronage that enabled a broad spectrum of musicians to be heard; without it, we might never have had the pleasure of so much musical variety.

I said I couldn't possibly mention all those who were influential but I can't resist flagging-up a few more names from a particularly rich period of musical creativity.

For starters, there was Richard Thompson. Having left Fairport Convention, he produced a challenging solo album, *Henry The Human Fly*, before going on to record with his then wife, Linda Peters. Their first offering, *I Want To See The Bright Lights Tonight*, was little short of a masterpiece, though never really figured on the radar. That has been pretty much the story of Richard Thompson's life. He is an unsung genius, a musician's musician and prolific writer. His songs have been covered by artists as diverse as Bonnie Raitt, REM, Alison Krauss, Michael Ball, The Corrs and Tom Jones; one song, 'The Dimming Of

The Day' has been covered no less than forty times. If you are shaking your head and saying 'Richard who?' then shame on you!

Free was a blues-rock band extraordinaire, fronted by Paul Rogers and lead guitarist Paul Kossoff (sadly departed). Their combination of talent was the perfect vehicle for delivering powerful anthemic riffs as in 'Alright Now' and 'Wishing Well'. After their second – and terminal – break-up, Rogers went on to form Bad Company. Following the death of Freddie Mercury, he toured briefly with Queen.

Jeff Lynne joined with Roy 'I Wish It Could Be Christmas Every Day' Wood to form Electric Light Orchestra, later named ELO. Somehow they managed to make orchestral string sections rock, something that defined their sound and is still the hallmark of Lynne's work.

And I should mention Yes, not a band I liked particularly but one that was constantly challenging, and one that I was force-fed by college mates. Likes Pink Floyd, they were at the sharp end of progressive rock, much of the inspiration for their varied output stemming from occasional member Rick Wakeman. If I was a little lukewarm about their music, I thought that artist Roger Dean's artwork on the Yes album sleeves was without parallel.

Who else? Graham Gouldman was only nineteen when he wrote 'For Your Love', a huge hit for the Yardbirds in 1965. He went on to form 10cc, those alchemists of the clever multi-layered songs. Ian Anderson, a man who could make a flute sound like the dawn chorus or spit out rock notes like a rabid dog, was the genius behind the totally unique Jethro Tull, a band that blurred pretty much every musical style by folding rock into jazz into traditional folk, classical and back again. The Bonzo Dog Doo-Dah Band, the clown princes of rock, have always been a tonic for me, constantly poking fun at society's stereotypes and always willing to mock the music establishment with hilarious vocals and caricatures of musical styles. They were led by funny men Viv Stanshall and Neil Innes, the latter a key contributor to *Monty Python's Flying Circus*.

Such was the quality of musicianship at the time that I could write this piece ten times over, each time with a totally different line-up of musical talent. Now, some forty-plus years since the release of *Tubular Bells*, it is all still very precious to me.

The really important thing is when this was happening. It was a time when creativity and imagination fashioned new thinking, new art and a new outlook for a generation. It was exciting, sexy and bloody good fun!

13

FISH, CHIPS AND GARLIC BREAD

THERE was just one remaining chore that I, plus the rest of Britain, needed to address before I could depart for Leeds. Having decimalised our currency two years previously, we were now voting to become members of the Common Market. I was generally in favour, believing that a unified Europe was more likely to be a peaceful one; the end of WW2 was little more than twenty years earlier and still very much in the memory of the governing generation.

Much has changed since then and the Eurocrats who now preside over the member states from their ivory towers in Brussels seem rather detached from their constituents. As I write, there is much debate as to whether we remain or leave the European Union (EU).

In my opinion, the organisation we joined which opened up our nations to trade has been superseded by an ambition to create a European superstate, about which I have many concerns. In this respect I find myself reflecting on the words of Winston Churchill. Post-WW2, he promoted the concept of a United Sates of Europe but with significant provisos:

'We help, we dedicate, we play our part, but we are not merged with and do not forfeit our insular or commonwealth character ... we are a separate, closely and specially-related ally and friend... It is only when plans for uniting Europe take a federal form that we ourselves cannot take part, because we cannot subordinate ourselves or the control of British policy to federal authorities.'

He also stated: '*We are with them, but not of them.*'

I do not view our nation as anything special or in some way superior to our fellow Europeans, but I place a lot of importance on cultural diversity and I fear this could be under threat from a European bloc superstate.

One inevitable (and I'm inclined to say unfortunate) side effect of our closer association with Europe is that we simultaneously loosened our ties to the Commonwealth, the very thing Churchill had warned against. Admittedly, the spectacle of the Union Jack being lowered in Commonwealth countries had become a fairly frequent event during the previous fifty years or so, but I now think that the whole business was a lost opportunity for all the parties involved. I can understand why these nations wanted their independence but I believe that if we had invested a lot more in terms of education, health and trade (and by that I mean fair trade), a true common wealth could have been achieved for the benefit of all. The simple fact that these nations were in totally different climatic and geological regions enabled us to trade in a huge variety of produce, thereby potentially creating sound economic links.

Unfortunately our patronising, Victorian attitudes toward these nations caused us to lose face, and left some of the former colonies floundering to find stability and their own identity in the modern world. I suspect that if all this had been handled with greater sensitivity and mutual respect, the Common Market's business might have appeared rather less attractive.

I am left in something of a quandary. I am British, therefore European, and in 1973 voted for stronger ties within a European league of nations. However, I become concerned when our sovereignty is compromised and the complexion of our society is ceded to a bureaucratic governance outside our shores. As a body, the EU now encompasses a far greater number of constituent parts. I worry that the imposition of commonality across such a diverse group of nations is damaging to the cultural diversity and, in some cases, the aspirations of its member states. I also fear that more dominant members have the opportunity to skew the workings of the Union in their favour at the cost of others.

I would suggest that the industrial make-up of the UK would look remarkably different now had we not joined. Whether that would be for better or for worse I have no idea; judging by current debate, it is a conundrum that challenges our leading economists and politicians. That said, they are never backward in coming forward to express their prejudicial views; the art of skewing is an irresistible temptation to those in power and with something to gain or lose!

14

STUDENT LIFE

STUDENT life didn't get off to the best start. Finding somewhere to live in Leeds proved difficult, and I faced the prospect of starting college without knowing my accommodation or my future house mates. So, on a grey autumnal afternoon I found myself in a small end-terrace house in Armley that had all the kerb appeal of a gun emplacement.

With the greatest respect to its citizens, I have to say that Armley was rather desolate back in the seventies. Many of the old brick terraces had been cleared for redevelopment that wasn't coming any time soon. There was also the forbidding dark outline of the Victorian gothic prison looming large on the skyline which did little to allay an all-round sense of despair.

I was first to arrive in our three-person household, so had the first experience of the hideous carpets, leaking toilet pedestal and damp musky odour. Fortunately my two house mates were cheerful West Country lads studying at Leeds University.

Our first week was overshadowed by our concerns about our landlady. We had no paperwork confirming our tenancy and no rent book, an arrangement she felt no need to change. *'Bugger that,'* we thought, and after a few weeks decided to do a moonlight flit to a Victorian terraced house in Headingley.

The new place was a dump but it was legit, with a rent book and a landlord who promised to correct all the property's many failings, though he never did. It came with another student, a scruffy, awkward individual from Sheffield, who smelled constantly of joss sticks. It was pretty clear from the outset that his reclusive Gothic tendencies would make him the black sheep of the household. His unpredictable mood swings, often fuelled by drink and goodness knows what else, eventually ended in his departure.

It was a strange place, a through-terrace with two addresses: Hall Grove at the front, which we used as the postal address, and Ebor Mount at the back, which we used for access. Stevenage New Town it wasn't, but the spacious proportions and modest garden suggested it had previously been the home of Victorian artisans rather than members of the working class.

In 1973, the terrace accommodated an eclectic range of tenants; our near neighbours included an Irish family, a Pakistani family, a young professional couple and a house full of student nurses. There was no obvious community spirit, just polite acknowledgements and healthy respect for one another's privacy. A nod, a smile or a hello – maybe just a little more than that in the direction of the nurses!

Internally the house was well-proportioned and provided decent accommodation, though ours had seen years of student action and was showing signs of not coping with the strain. It had a motley collection of furniture and floor coverings. I particularly remember the carpet in the common/dining room, one of those contoured types on which the three-dimensional pattern had long since been trampled flat in all but the most inaccessible locations and had been reinforced by many a culinary spillage.

From the small kitchen a flight of stairs led down to a cellar containing an impenetrable mountain of junk. It had no light, which discouraged further exploration. Had light ever illuminated the space, I suspect it would have revealed a scene reminiscent of *Steptoe and Son* meeting *The Addams Family*.

My room on the ground floor was large, with furnishings from the nineteen-twenties and thirties, including a wardrobe that was large enough to qualify for its own postcode. My jeans and shirt, plus one change of clothes, hung small, crumpled and sad inside its cavernous quarters.

Despite its obvious shortcomings, the place had two great advantages: it was closer to both the university and the school of landscape architecture, and it was near a number of useful shops. There was a general store specialising in out-of-date Lyons' fruit pies and including amongst its staff a cat, which was often curled up in open tubs of dried foodstuffs. There was an off licence/corner shop that was open 24/7, a magnificent little bakery whose warm fresh produce was irresistible on a chilly winter's morning, and a launderette. Sadly the bakery and the launderette were demolished while we lived in the area, a portent of things to come and symptomatic of a new generation that would have less respect for constancy and individuality as it ran headlong towards the shopping mall, home technology and the pizza-delivery man!

I think the challenge of being a student has changed a great deal over the intervening forty years, particularly in financial terms. In 1973 the nation was some way from the nightmare of student loans and their attendant misery and divisiveness. We subsisted on grants; a raggedy-arsed student studying a classics subject, for example, could pretty much get through college with a pad and a biro. Now everyone needs a computer and a plethora of hi-tech gizmos to go with it, not to mention the obligatory smart phones, all of which are easy pickings for petty thieves and burglars.

I realised this when I revisited my old Leeds stamping grounds and found metal bars adorning the windows and doors of many of the terraced houses. The cosmopolitan mix of families and students that I had enjoyed had gone; most of the houses were occupied by students, reflecting the landlords' grab for the highest possible returns on their investments.

⊙ ⊙ ⊙

My first term was a disaster, what with accommodation problems and having to adopt a new student way of life. I managed to weather the storm and duly turned up for work at Stevenage a week or two before Christmas.

Those few weeks back at work coincided with a major national crisis. For several months Prime Minister Ted Heath had been at loggerheads with the National Union of Mineworkers (NUM) about pay restraint and the miners had responded by working to rule. In other words, the lights went out. Coal supply to the power stations dwindled so much that on the 31st of December 1973 a three-day working week was imposed to conserve stocks for as long as possible. What on earth had happened to the optimism of the sixties?

It pains me to say it, but the trade unions – or at least their chosen representatives – had a lot to answer for at this time. I've always had a lot of respect for miners, given the dangers involved in their work, but they precipitated this particular crisis. It proved to be the first of many such occasions in the seventies where the unrealistic claims made by militant shop stewards and conveners would cripple industry.

Probably the worst of these occurred at British Leyland (BL), our last remaining major car manufacturer. By the middle of the decade it seemed to be dominated by Derek Robinson aka Red Robbo, a self-proclaimed communist. His unreasonable claims and strike actions eventually brought the company to its knees and in 1975 the government was forced to nationalise it to save jobs. It was as if the unions, born out of a genuine social need to protect the working classes from exploitation and the excesses of capitalism, had become the bastard children of greed.

The whole sorry saga was little short of a national disaster, but you know we Brits – always ready to raise a laugh in a crisis. On this occasion, the honours fell to The Strawbs. Their song '(You Don't Get Me) I'm Part Of The Union' was clearly a send up, but one that ironically backfired when the union movement adopted it as an anthem and sang it regularly on picket lines.

With all this going on and inflation winking at double figures, the country was in deep doo-doo. I reckoned it was a pretty good time to be a hairy, layabout, union-card waving student cocooned in the cosy world of academia.

⊙⊙⊙

Come the spring of 1974, I started to get the hang of student life. Feeling more at one with my new persona, I enjoyed the rest of that first academic year, got to grips with my college work and generally felt more comfortable and relaxed, most frequently at the university union.

The union was a pretty relaxed place. There were certain places within its walls where little groups of hairy, denim-encrusted students huddled, and from which occasionally wisps of sweet-smelling smoke rose serpent-like to the ceiling. My grandad's Old Holborn never smelt like that! These guys were obviously struggling with their grant money because they had to share a roll-up between them – though it was a big 'un. Still, they seemed quite happy and extremely mellow.

In addition to providing the cheapest drink in town, the student union was also the place to find my beloved rock music both in its record shop and at the regular concerts. At that time, rock bands used university/college towns and cities to ply their trade so there was plenty of opportunity to see some great acts. I recall seeing Kiki Dee, Bad Company, Traffic, The Chieftains, Pentangle and Fairport Convention, but I'm ashamed to say I didn't really take full advantage of what was on offer. Why the hell didn't I go and see Queen and Steely Dan? My only defence is that bands toured so regularly I was confident I'd have other opportunities to see them. In the case of Queen and Dan, I was proved wrong.

Sadly, I also missed out on seeing Sandy Denny who, as a former member of Fairport Convention, is generally regarded as a co-founder of the folk-rock style of music. It seems she visited not once but three times during the four years I was in Leeds. Given the chance today, I'd willingly walk across burning coals to see her and hear her beautiful voice, but alas that can't happen. She passed away in 1978, aged thirty-one, just one year after I left college. She was another casualty of a gifted generation of musicians who were often consumed and destroyed by the intensity of their talent and the demands this placed upon them.

Whilst the union was pretty much the hub of student recreation and entertainment, it was by no means our only venue for such activities. Headingley was, and no doubt still is, the student ghetto for Leeds.

Back in the early seventies, it was well stocked with pubs and a couple of cinemas. The Royal Park pub was just a few minutes down the road, and Friday and Saturday evenings were karaoke night (only they weren't, because karaoke hadn't been invented). What they had was a piano player whose task was to accompany inebriated punters who, after ten pints of Tetley's best bitter, thought they were Bill Hayley, Elvis Presley or Pavarotti or all three rolled into one. When we weren't watching some paralytic, incoherent interpretation of Elvis Pavarotti, we would gather round the Atari Ping-Pong table-tennis game. Remember those? Mind-numbingly boring, yet somehow addictive.

The pub scene back then might as well have been 140 years ago rather than just forty. I recall the Lord Nelson in Armley where late arrivals were greeted with a smoke-filled microclimate that scorched the back of the throat and seriously impaired visibility. Having said that, the impact on one's ability to see across the room was not all bad news; if you were as bad at darts as I was, it levelled the playing field a bit. In the Nelson you could have had Stevie Wonder in your team and not felt particularly disadvantaged.

Another quaint tradition of this rather seedy establishment was the men-only bar. Unthinkable now, but not totally uncommon in the 1970s. Indeed, many years would pass before the Nelson's misogynistic, bronchially-challenged clientele were legally banned from smoking and its management prevented from excluding people on the basis of their sex. I believe last orders was called some time ago on the Nelson, and that it subsequently became an Indian restaurant. I guess, if nothing else, it should now curry favour with the ladies!

In summer 1974 I returned to Leeds with considerably more confidence than when I'd made my entry twelve months earlier. The departure of our hairy housemate had left a vacancy within the house that was taken by the girlfriend of one of the other tenants. She was athletic, very pretty and was going to Carnegie Teacher Training College, as it then was. Her presence brought a palpable calm to the place and we became a noticeably more balanced household.

The older I become, the more I am convinced that the world would be a far better place if we had more women in positions of influence. They have a better understanding of values and a more rational perspective on life, especially in moments of tension and confrontation. As a man, I am ashamed by the irrefutable fact that it is the arrogance and insecurity of the male ego that has perpetuated the subjugation of women, whether it be in West Yorkshire, Timbuktu or anywhere else in the entire world. Anyway, in our red-brick terraced house in Headingley in 1974 equality reigned, and our new member quickly became a very welcome addition. Not only that, as a unit we now had a member in all three of the major colleges in Leeds, something that significantly expanded our circle of friends. So, in order to cement our social standing we bowed to the inevitable: a student house party.

It went something like this:

Step one: compile a reel-to-reel tape of the coolest, hippest party music – Doobie Brothers, Rod Stewart, Free, Rolling Stones, Stevie Wonder, etc, etc.

Step two: purchase a huge cask of beer called something like Old Yorkshire Knee Trembler, plus one bottle of Blue Nun for the ladies. The cask was purchased from a highly dubious source operating out of a railway arch near the station.

Step three: clear the decks for revelry. It wasn't as if we could inflict much damage to the fabric of the house; that had been taken care of by many years of total neglect and a steady stream of head-banging student occupants.

Come 11pm on party night, there was bad news followed by more bad news. First, our supply of Knee Trembler was running low and the booze table was now populated by nothing but bottles of cheap supermarket cider contributed by our tight-fisted guests. Secondly, our celebration had not gone unnoticed by the local police who appeared in the form of two smiley-faced plods and a cheery, *'What's going on 'ere then?'* or words to that effect. Obviously they had seen it all before because Headingley was pretty much the epicentre of student socialising and partying.

After a quick shufty behind the saucepans in the kitchen, where they discovered dust rather than illegal substances, and having declined our offer of a swift half of Knee Trembler, they left with a polite request that we keep the noise down. To be quite honest, it was a bit of a disappointment. We were trying so hard to look like 'men behaving badly' and seriously rock 'n' roll, only to have them leave thinking we were a sad bunch of pussycats!

The party ended at about 1.00am when we forcibly ejected some inebriated bloke (whom nobody knew), but not before he drank the contents of the keg. We tipped it on its end to drain what was left and out poured something resembling lumpy cold coffee. He snatched it from us before weaving his way into the night, regaling us as he went with a torrent of abuse.

The beginning of the third year saw us in a different property back in Armley. Victorian values would suggest we had moved downmarket, swapping our artisan property for a worker's back-to-back, but it was a clean, modestly refurbished house and rather more conducive to study. The business end of college life was now becoming a whole lot more serious for all of us, and for me it proved to be the most exciting and rewarding of my four years in Leeds.

It was customary to offer a few third-year landscape students the opportunity to work with their contemporaries from other environmental/building disciplines on a series of projects designed to run for most of the academic year. Having worked with architects in Stevenage, I was keen to take this opportunity. My fellow students were rather more reticent about the prospect on account of the course tutor, one Dr Theo Matoff.

An ultra-pragmatic Canadian, whose name seemed to strike terror into many students (and I suspect some members of staff), he had a reputation for direct speaking and crap-cutting. As we would soon find out, he was totally without compromise, vehemently intolerant of indulgent waffle and demanded that students be able to justify every aspect of their actions in resolving design problems. It was a philosophy he captured concisely in his oft-used expression, '*Sort it out, for Christ's sake. There's people out there in the rain.*'

He proved to be every bit the task master we feared, but I think those of us who took up the challenge agreed that the experience made us far better designers.

Three other landscape students also opted for this alternative. We transferred our stuff down to the interdisciplinary studio in the School of Architecture and joined forces with a couple of architectural students to work on two projects.

The first required us to go into the community of Hemingbrough, a small village just outside Selby in the middle of the area designated to be opened up for the Selby coalfield. Our task was to work with the community via the parish council and use open meetings to demonstrate how the village could be developed to accommodate an enlarged population, should that be necessary.

It is worth taking a minute to reflect on this, not because of our input but because it was an interesting episode and a turning point in attitudes to coal. The mine began producing in 1983, with a prediction that it could continue to do so for forty years. It was high-quality coal that could be extracted cleanly without the need for unsightly slag heaps. Arguably it was the world's most advanced mine – but it was developed too late.

The whole project lasted barely twenty years, was rarely profitable; it eventually succumbed to a slump in coal prices, political posturing and fears that it would cause subsidence to the Vale of York and increase the risk of flooding. It was the last gasp for deep-shaft mining and the start of a new era in the way we would seek to generate energy.

As for all those workers who were set to descend on Hemingbrough, they didn't come. The vast majority of them commuted from other declining coalfields as far distant as Newcastle and Wakefield. I guess that kind of nullified our efforts; nevertheless it was a useful, if at times terrifying, exercise in public consultation and speaking.

For our second challenge, the polytechnic entered our team in a worldwide competition, the goal of which was to demonstrate how a small community of about ten families might use a piece of land to achieve a level of self-sufficiency and maximise the location to produce food and energy through the use of green, environmentally friendly and sustainable practices. The competition, EPROM'76, was promoted by the Rideau Institute of Canada, an organisation developed to promote green ideologies, and the selected site was in Ontario.

We settled on an analytical approach: we would research the location as much as was physically possible, then justify our suggestions in detail to demonstrate our understanding of the site. The work was completed and sent off to Canada. In April, during the Easter holiday, I received a telegram from one of the architects involved with the project.

Just thought you'd like to know that all those hours on Eprom have paid off – yes, we won it! Now, scream!

Yes, heard yesterday by telegram and thus mentally stunned! ... Theo couldn't believe it either!!!

Oh Geesus (sic) Christ...

See you Monday.

It was an exciting time and crowned two enjoyable terms working within an interdisciplinary team. The thoughts and ideas of others are often inspirational; at college we were continually motivated by Doc Matoff, and occasionally by the eminent architect Patrick Nuttgens, director of the polytechnic. He possessed a razor-sharp mind and an uncanny ability to ask incisive questions about a subject he had known nothing about just five minutes earlier.

At the time of his death, in March of 2004, *The Independent's* obituary described him as:

A man of many accomplishments – architect, gifted artist, writer, scholar, broadcaster, pundit and presenter, raconteur – he was, at bottom, a teacher; inspired and inspiring, lively and probing and ever challenging.

⊙⊙⊙

And so to the greatest challenge: my final year at Leeds. In many respects it was the college itself that posed the biggest problem in that the schools of landscape and architecture were now housed under one roof in Brunswick House. This was new, but as yet incomplete, accommodation. We had been made aware of this change but it was still a culture shock. Previously we had been housed in old buildings where students were allowed – even invited – to personalise their work spaces, giving rise to a colourful and stimulating atmosphere. In the sterile, sanitised monstrosity of Brunswick House, such actions were regarded as wanton acts of vandalism.

The whole place seemed to stifle any form of creativity; it was also physically stifling. People often recall the summer of 1976 as being a scorcher but 1977 wasn't far behind. The heat highlighted problems with the new building, where a combination of dodgy air-con and sealed windows made life very uncomfortable. These and its many other faults were seized upon by *Fresh Today*, the paper published by the Leeds Poly Union.

The Polytechnic's newest building is fast becoming the biggest white elephant in Leeds. Situated in Brunswick Terrace, behind the Merrion Centre, it has been designed to house the Schools of Architecture and Constructional Studies. This is somewhat ironical because during the recent heavy rain the building started letting in water, the ground floor isn't strong enough to take the machinery that is to be installed, and there are only a handful of toilets for the five hundred students.

These are just a few of the problems in the block, which was to be the first of three phases. The third phase has now been abandoned and building of the second has just started, two years behind schedule.

It was not surprising that many students (including me) tended to go there as little as possible. Though I didn't know it at the time, my career was destined to outlive this awful edifice, a fact brought to my attention a couple of years ago when I was presented with a small packet of rubble apparently rescued from the recently-demolished Brunswick House. I imagine the decision to sell the site was an easy one given that it occupied a prime city-centre location; the 'money men' no doubt perceived it as a golden goose rather than the white elephant it had become even before its completion.

Fortunately the first term was almost entirely devoted to writing my final dissertation, so I had no great need to visit the Brunswick hothouse other than to attend tutorials. I knew the dissertation would be difficult for someone like me who preferred Pictionary to Scrabble, and there never seemed to be enough time. In the blink of an eye, Christmas came and went and I was on a train heading back to Leeds knowing I still had a lot to do to finish my written work.

Winter quickly turned to spring. I needed to meet the deadline for completing my dissertation before going forward with my final design project, both of which centred on inner-city housing regeneration. Perhaps that seems a strange choice for someone whose working life so far had been predominantly in new towns.

I managed to finish everything and arrived at the day when students came face to face with the visiting examiners. It was pretty nerve-racking stuff; a warm sunny day combined with inadequate air-con at Brunswick House tested even the most confident amongst us. But I managed to get by and then waited nervously for the results to be posted on the notice board.

It was late in the afternoon before they appeared. As I saw my name amongst those who had passed, a huge sense of relief ran through my body. It's a sensation very difficult to describe.

⊙⊙⊙

Leeds was good for me. I started my training there with a few years' office experience, which proved a great advantage in that I was already attuned to my professional destiny, but there was more to it than that. I was confronted with new design challenges and experienced the world beyond the comfortable new-town existence that had been my life until then.

I was also exposed to new ideas and concepts, of which there were many back in the mid-seventies. Planting design in particular was being influenced by the experiences of other countries, notably Holland, and this was being incorporated into fresh thinking in the UK.

Outside the profession there was also much to ponder. The ten golden years of music, heralded by The Beatles' *Revolver* album, was spluttering to its demise. Bands continued to progress, but some started to produce work that was seriously self-indulgent whilst others became pale imitations of their former selves.

There was worse to come. Complacency turned to navel gazing and during the hiatus we were attacked by the ugly sound of angry young men – or was it the angry sound of ugly young men? Either way, it was the most God-awful musical disaster ever vented upon mankind.

Punk: the anti-Christ of all that is musically sacred. Suddenly, but fortunately only briefly, talent was replaced by anarchy, attitude and vulgarity. I hated it. It even made me fall out temporarily with John Peel, who championed these rebellious renegades of rock, though I don't suppose JP lost too much sleep about that. Mercifully some semblance of normality returned within a couple of years, but nothing was ever quite the same again.

On the plus side, people seemed to be more mindful of their environment. Fuel efficiency in vehicles and the possibility of recycling were being considered by a much wider section of the population. It looked as if we were heading in the right direction – so what went wrong? It is a conundrum I shall return to later in my scrapbook but, as a fresh-faced college graduate in 1977, I was looking forward with an open mind and a lot of optimism.

I had achieved a qualification in a career I cared about. I had a job to return to, a piece of paper that told the world I had a Diploma in Landscape Architecture, and I hoped to do something positive with my skills. The ordeal of passing the final professional examination and becoming a fully-fledged practitioner lay ahead, but I decided I'd put that off for a few years.

15

LOVE AMONGST THE ROUNDABOUTS

I returned to Stevenage in the summer of 1977 and was rewarded with a healthy pay rise, commensurate with my new professional status. However, there was a perceptible change at the corporation and storm clouds were gathering.

Stevenage Development Corporation had been growing the town in accordance with a master plan for more than thirty years when suddenly there were rumours of closure. It was almost as if someone had gone into work one morning and noticed that nearly all the demarcated land had been developed.

The proverbial hit the fan a couple of months after my return when the staff were summoned to a meeting in the nearby sports and social centre. The lady chairman and the chief officers sat in front of us at a long table suitably draped with a black cloth (the table, not the chairman), and announced that there was a programme in place to phase out the corporation. It would be wound down fairly gently, but all members of staff were free to seek employment elsewhere. I was no longer compelled to work out my two-year agreement; only time would tell if this would work to my advantage or not.

It turned out to be a very short wait. By late autumn, Milton Keynes Development Corporation had offered me a job in their landscape team. By extending my commitment to the new-town movement, I was able to pay my two year dues and still move away from Stevenage.

I'd enjoyed my time there. I will always be grateful to Gordon Patterson for the job opportunity and also to my colleagues, from whom I learned a great deal. My departure was forced by circumstances outside my control, but there are times when you know you've got to make a fresh start and this was one of them.

⊙⊙⊙

Job interviews can be counted upon to send your nerves jangling. They offer a brief opportunity to make a decision that will affect your career and possibly change the direction of your whole life. Sometimes you know immediately that a job is not for you; at other times, you feel comfortable and excited about the possibility of a new employer. The problems start when you have doubts at the back of your mind and, no matter how objective you try to be, you can't decide one way or the other.

I'd spent a year at college researching the condition of our inner cities and how their decline might be addressed, so Milton Keynes was not a particularly logical place to start. That aside, it was a Mecca for landscape architects and to have it on one's CV was worth a lot of brownie points. But would Milton Keynes have a positive impact on my career and my personal life? That answer came quickly; I was engaged by the spring and, come September, a very happily married man. You have no idea what might happen when you change jobs!

My life was now going places I had only ever dreamt of. I was in a permanent relationship with an attractive and intelligent woman and we were enjoying one another's company, going to concerts, shopping together, doing everything together.

There was some memorable music to celebrate this special moment in my life. Soft rock – or yacht rock as it is now often called – provided some melodic, gentle sounds via Toto, Hall and Oates and Foreigner. Fleetwood Mac had re-emerged a few years previously with the inclusion of American duo Lindsey Buckingham and Stevie Nicks. In doing so they morphed from a raunchy, sweaty, blues rock band to become purveyors of slick niceness. Their *Fleetwood Mac* album sold copies by the shed load, as did the follow-up, *Rumours*. I was seduced by their shiny new image, but once I'd licked off the sweet coating I yearned for the sanctuary of Peter Green's earlier manifestation of the band with its blues' classics.

Like Fleetwood Mac, the Bee Gees also enjoyed a renaissance after they contributed to the soundtrack of *Saturday Night Fever*. The brilliant Gerry Rafferty had recently released his *City to City* album, including the imperious 'Baker Street', and Dire Straits were 'the sultans of swing'. If that were not enough, the beautiful, talented and mysterious Kate Bush had arrived on the scene performing cartwheels in a white-lace dress, pouting her cherry-red lips and singing wistful romantic songs in homage to past times, notably 'Wuthering Heights' and 'The Man With The Child In His Eyes'.

Punk rock had morphed into New Wave and was counterbalanced by a culture of sequin-spangled glam rockers and New Romantics. Yin had met yang! But in all this joyful musical hysteria there was one consequence I hadn't considered: the impact my new love life would have on my record collection.

My collection of Steely Dan albums were now rubbing alphabetical shoulders with Shakatak and Barbara Streisand. Earth, Wind and Fire had somehow sneaked in between Bob Dylan and Fairport Convention. I really must have been in love.

And remember Cliff Richard? He was *still* singing (will he ever give up?). He added insult to injury by showing up in Milton Keynes to film a video for his song 'Wired For Sound'. How was it possible that the guy whose toe-tapping ditties that had echoed from our Disc Jockey Junior some twenty years earlier could still be selling records by the million in an age when Sid Vicious was courting popular culture by spewing out 'I Am The Anti-Christ'? But this was Britain and, notwithstanding our many faults as a nation, we are a pretty diverse and tolerant bunch, thank God!

⊙⊙⊙

The summer of '78 passed in a flash as we arranged a wedding and honeymoon. With all the formalities completed, we flew to Edinburgh. After a couple of days in a turreted Rapunzel-esque pile, we set off on the second leg of our honeymoon to a hotel near Oban, about which my abiding memory is the awful nylon sheets. Good old Brentford Nylons, the epitome of all that was naff about seventies' Britain.

Funnily enough, the other day I stumbled on an old copy of the *Daily Express* in which I discovered an ad for Brentford Nylons. In addition to the usual bedding items, there were thumbnail images and alluring descriptions for nightwear fashioned from *cosy simulated brushed nylon.* The gentlemen's section featured 'nylon PJs', and a 'quilted-nylon smoking jacket'. Who the hell wore a smoking jacket in the seventies?

There must have been major problems with wearing nylon jammies and swathing yourself in nylon sheets. One warm, restless summer's night and you'd probably have generated enough friction to deliver third-degree burns – or run the risk of being struck by lightning!

Having done threadbare Edinburgh baronial and traditional Scottish-nylon luxury, our final destination was the Kyle of Lochalsh Hotel. Perched on the edge of the loch, with the promise of stunning views across to the Isle of Skye, the view was spectacular but not how I'd pictured it. I had misinterpreted the 'Skye Boat Song', the first verse of which is:

Speed, bonnie boat, like a bird on the wing,
Onward, the sailors cry,
Carry the lad that's born to be king
Over the sea to Skye.

I draw your attention to the fourth line: *Over the sea to Skye.* I had expected to observe the Isle of Skye as a distant interruption on a misty horizon but instead it filled the view from our window. It was beautiful, but not what I'd expected. I decided that Sir Harold Boulton, the Victorian English gentleman responsible for the lyrics, had, like me, never ever actually been to Lochalsh. Over the sea, my arse!

The other day I revisited the history of the Jacobite rebellions and found that my dismissal was a total misconception. Bonnie Prince Charlie's retreat from Culloden was a fairly protracted affair; he eluded the attention of the Duke of Cumberland for five months before leaving the mainland not directly to Skye but to the Hebridean island of Eriskay. His pursuers closed in on him two months later and, with the help of Flora McDonald, he escaped back to Skye, hence *Over the sea (back) to Skye*. Apparently the escape saw him dress up as Miss McDonald's maid, which paints a very different picture to that of William Wallace, the other notable rebellious Scot. With BPC's long, curly blond locks he wouldn't have looked so much Highland savage as Lily Savage!

He was eventually rescued by the French – who else? – at the Isle of Raasay and that was the end of the Jacobite rebellions, other than in 1967 when football fans decided to dismantle the Wembley goalposts after witnessing their team defeat England,.

The following year, my wife and I bought our first home. Many of you will have your own memories of this experience, some good and some not so good. When it came to pitching for a mortgage, I felt pretty confident. We were earning identical professional salaries in jobs that were totally secure, and we already had a deposit. Consequently it came as a shock when our local Halifax Building Society manager bounced our application based on his own opinion rather than any approved financial vetting methodology. So much for *Always giving you extra*.

We lost the battle but not the war. We eventually secured a mortgage and moved into a nearly-new, linked-detached house in Great Linford. One of several villages subsumed into the fabric of the new city, its rural charms demanded a rather more traditional design approach than much of the new housing elsewhere. It was vastly different to our previous corporation house on an estate called Coffee Hall, where the grey, brutal terraces looked rather more stalag than arcadian.

We couldn't have picked a better moment to set up home in MK. The shopping centre had just opened its doors for the first time, and there were shiny new things to buy from stores like John Lewis, Habitat and Marks and Spencer. It was officially opened in June 1979 by our new, first-ever lady Prime Minister, Mrs Thatcher, who had won a convincing victory in the general election a month earlier. We were in the building at the time and she bade us good morning as she shuffled past in that rather infuriating busy-bee manner she had.

Given that the Queen was to visit MK later in the year, it seemed rather strange that Mrs T had the honour of opening the shopping centre. I can only surmise that there was some political posturing going on, the mandarins at MK no doubt trying to protect the funding stream to which they had become accustomed. The previous Labour Secretary of State for the Environment, Peter Shore, had been of the opinion that the new-town programme was being funded at the expense of London.

With my new marital status, a secure job and several years MK experience behind me, it seemed the right time to face something I'd been putting off: my final professional exam. This took the form of an interview, the verbal torture being administered by two seasoned professionals, and for this I had to travel to Birmingham.

I remember the day very clearly. At the time, England were one down in the Ashes test series having lost the first test at Trent Bridge. To all intents and purposes they were dead and buried in the third test at Headingley until an insouciant Ian Botham clubbed a cavalier 149 not out. Might a slender lead of 129 be enough for England to actually win? As I arrived in Brum, Bob Willis and co were starting to rip through the Aussie's batting order – but I had to remain focussed on the task ahead.

All interviewees were allocated a time for their interview and someone had to be last – but why did it have to be me? A 4.30pm slot meant I had about five hours to kill.

A dozen of us gathered in a large, featureless room where the chairs had been placed around the walls, dentist-waiting-room fashion. We sat, gazing blankly at an unmarked spot in the centre of the floor, avoiding eye contact as this would have destroyed our concentration, caused a loss of focus leading to failure of the examination, loss of professional status, social fall from grace, a life of crime and homelessness... I couldn't take too much of that, so I returned to my car to listen to the test match.

It was about 4pm when I went back in expecting there to be only one or two fellow sufferers remaining. There were considerably more, all still hypnotised by the magic spot in the centre of the room. To break the ice, which was glacial by now, I blurted out, 'I don't suppose anyone's particularly bothered, but England have just won the test match.'

I would have had a better response if we'd actually been in a dentist's waiting room, awaiting the removal of wisdom teeth. 'They're running late,' came the rather oblique response.

Feeling suitably chastised, I sat down and joined the spot-watchers. Sure enough, they were running very late; by the time I was eventually summoned, it was clear that the tormentors were as hacked-off as the rest of us.

The interviewee's chair was lower than the rest, something I didn't notice until I sat down. As a result, I plummeted rather than sat and kicked over a bin that had been strategically placed to catch the unaware. I managed to regain my composure and somehow got through the ordeal – and passed!

From eleven-plus failure to a fully-fledged landscape architect with letters after my name was an ambition fulfilled, though the confidence I gained did not spill over into job satisfaction. I had asked myself if Milton Keynes would be a good career move; the answer was most certainly yes, but I was never really comfortable there and frequently found myself out of step with office culture. It was no one's fault; I was a square peg in a round hole. Churning out planting schemes time after time for housing developments and sections of the road system was rather like rolling out environmental wallpaper.

I started to realise that I am more comfortable as a designer when I'm trying to overcome inherent landscape/environmental problems. I am less comfortable when given a blank sheet and told to come up with fresh design ideas. I guess that is something that's always likely to haunt a confirmed introvert.

The following spring an opportunity arose with Cleveland County Council in Middlesbrough. My colleagues probably thought I was crazy wanting to leave the gentle Buckinghamshire countryside for the industrially scarred north east, but it presented an opportunity to be involved in the type of work I'd trained for. I wasn't fazed by the idea of working in the centre of Middlesbrough because I was familiar with the beautiful North Yorkshire countryside that lay to the south of it.

Any reassurance I needed came at my interview. From the sixth floor of the building I looked out across a panoramic view of heavy industry, with its concentration of bleak utilitarian structures punctuated with cooling towers and tall flaming stacks, but beyond that I could see the Eston Hills and Roseberry Topping, a conical hill that dominates the northern edge of the North Yorkshire Moors National Park. It looked dramatic and exciting. Just a few days later I was told I'd got the job, and my long association with the new-town movement was at an end.

From cradle to career I'd lived the rather privileged lifestyle created by the new-town communities, but my family ties in South Yorkshire ensured that I was also exposed to the harsh realities of the British industrial township. Even as a kid I was sensitive to the environmental chasm that separated suburban Hatfield or Welwyn Garden City from the northern towns and cities such as Doncaster, Sheffield and Leeds.

The cause was gaining momentum; professional journals were now focussing on transforming murky Victorian back-to-backs and reclaiming colliery tips rather than on prestigious (and often over-indulgent) projects in far-flung parts of the world. I wanted to be part of that cause.

On a damp day in June, nearly four years after arriving, we loaded up our possessions and left the tree-lined city of roundabouts for 'Steel Town', home of the parmo and birthplace of Brian Clough and Chris Rea. Were we venturing towards a new and happy phase in our lives or on 'The Road To Hell'?

16

BRITAIN AT WAR

AT that time an event occurred that I really never expected to see: squaddies boarding the *QEII* at Southampton and waving farewell to loved ones. Surely that only happened in old newsreels?

The Falklands crisis had been dominating the news during the early months of 1982, and in April Argentinian armed forces invaded the islands. For the first time in my life, other than the ongoing disquiet in Northern Ireland, British troops were deployed in a major military conflict. Having enjoyed thirty years of post-war peace, I found it disturbing and again asked myself the question, '*Could I have done that if called upon?*' These were my fellow countrymen putting themselves directly into harm's way for the security of the realm in the same way they had in 1914 and 1939.

The prelude was a series of air attacks on the Falklands' airfield, designed to disable its use by the Argentinians. You will, I'm sure, remember the late Michael Hanrahan's broadcast from the aircraft carrier HMS *Hermes* following the first airborne attack. Prevented for security reasons from actually stating how many planes were involved, he reassured viewers by stating, 'I counted them all out, and I counted them all back.'

Britain's military might, which I'd always believed to be invincible given the victory achieved in WW2, eventually prevailed – but not before a series of bloody incidents and disasters conveyed by vivid TV news reports.

Other than seeing footage of America's disastrous campaign in Vietnam, my generation's interpretation of war was largely based on poor-quality film footage and a mindset that was detached from the real horrors of military engagement. Now the theatre of war was immediate, graphic, in colour and in our homes. It was altogether different and considerably more shocking.

On the 2 May, Margaret Thatcher ordered an attack on the Argentine battle cruiser *Belgrano*, despite it being outside an exclusion zone she had imposed as a warning to Argentinian naval movements. At the time it was sailing away from the zone and effectively posed no threat to British forces. The vessel was torpedoed and sunk by the destroyer HMS *Conqueror* with considerable loss of life, an act for which Thatcher would later be severely criticised, though she vehemently defended her actions by pointing out that it nullified the Argentinian navy, which was true in that it took no further part in the war. To me it seemed to be an unwarranted, wilful act of aggression, but these days I'm less hasty in my condemnation of those who make decisions where the outcome will inevitably result in loss of life, whether of the enemy or fellow countrymen. It is not a position I could even contemplate.

In the post-war analysis, there were two aspects I found more than a little disturbing. The first was something I've just mentioned: the very public interrogation of Thatcher. I'm not saying it was unjust or misplaced, but I'd never seen a British Prime Minister subjected to that level of aggressive questioning before. It is a pretty common occurrence these days, but I'd be very surprised if the BBC possesses crackly old tapes of radio interviews where Churchill was exposed to such hostile cross-examination.

The other point, and something not disclosed until later, was that the whole operation was hampered by some strategic foul-ups and, perhaps even more disturbingly, by some serious equipment failures. It seems that all the elements were present for a monumental defeat, and it is primarily down to the professionalism and adaptability of the RAF, together with the troops on the ground, that this outcome was avoided.

17

MOVING WITH THE TIMES

I'M sorry if this sounds a little naff, but moving north felt very much like coming home. I had enjoyed family connections in the Doncaster area from being a child, and my brother was already living in North Yorkshire having started the exodus in 1974.

The four years at college in Leeds, plus my time at Milton Keynes, meant I had been exiled from my home town of Hatfield for the best part of a decade, during which time it had changed to such an extent it now felt alien and remote. Even the street where I was born and raised had no hold on me. Virtually all the neighbours I'd grown up with had either moved on or passed away, leaving my folks in their semi-detached bastion of nostalgia and familiarity in a street of strangers. It just wasn't the same and, as it turned out, it wasn't too long before my parents also joined the migration north.

Our new home, a Georgian terraced house in the village of Brompton, was very different to the property we had left behind in Milton Keynes. It was more like the terraced houses I'd lived in at Leeds than any previous manifestation of my closeted new town existence.

I'd never lived in a village before, so where better to begin our familiarisation than the local pub, a litmus test of a community? There were four to choose from but we focussed our attentions on the Black Swan, a place I'd visited when staying with my brother and his family some years earlier.

I remembered it as a rustic establishment caught up in a time warp, where beer was served from an enamel jug by a delightful old chap who appeared to be Father Christmas's doppelgänger. I dreamed, rather optimistically as it turned out, of cosy winter nights drinking fine ale with Santa beside a roaring fire. Those ideas were in ruins before we set foot in the place. As we approached, I noticed that the old insignia of the Black Swan had been replaced by a bland board announcing The Village Inn and the choice of typeface was more Hewlett Packard than Ye Olde Country Pub. We entered rather more in hope than expectation, and our fears were soon realised.

Gone was the quaint ambience, replaced by dubious patterned carpets and even more dubious mock-wood wall panelling. The eccentric barman had also gone, his trusty enamel jug replaced by a set of electric pumps whose fizzy, tasteless beer can be found the length and breadth of the land. The seventies and eighties quest to rip the heart and soul from our public houses had claimed another victim.

Sometime later, the long-planned and long-awaited alterations to The Village Inn began and for a while we had to go without our genial, if somewhat tasteless, pint. The changes saw it evolve into a pub-restaurant and B&B, which looked good for the village as it clearly couldn't exist the way it was.

The goose, or perhaps I should say the Black Swan, had long since been cooked; its seventies' makeover had smothered its original features in mediocrity. I worry that we often sacrifice the character and idiosyncrasies of our public houses to pursue the gastro-pub, those places where dainty portions garnished by Interflora are served on plates the size of Stoke-on-Trent, and where chips (sorry, *pommes frites*) are offered in tiny copper buckets.

But this is just one of the many reincarnations to have befallen the British pub, inflicted by a combination of individual landlords and conglomerate PLCs. We've been subjected to everything from the eighties' revival, with chrome, neon and mirror balls, to the Irish bar strewn with brooms, rusty pans and Celtic detritus that suggest Ireland is populated entirely by tinkers and little, red-bearded men dressed in green fustian tunics.

That reminds me of a constructive adaptation of a pub or bar I found when on holiday on the beautiful Connemara coast. In a village called Cleggan, one of the local bars doubled as a grocery store. Here you could stock up on comestibles whilst enjoying a pint, which for someone who dislikes shopping as much as I do is a definite bonus. It is, I'm sure, something we should be exploring in rural communities around the UK where village shops have been disappearing like lemmings over a cliff.

About a year later, The Village Inn opened its doors for business once more. The superficiality of the seventies' makeover had gone but the place, at least to me, seemed to have lost its soul. No amount of restyling could recapture its original glory. In just twenty years, scrubbed floors, good ale and *hygge* had been replaced by brown furniture, mixed grill and hen parties. However, I appreciate that these establishments must move with the times, even if I sometimes struggle to do so!

18

IF MUSIC BE THE FOOD OF LOVE, PLAY ON...

AS the eighties progressed, we baby boomers had to face up to the very real prospect that life might not begin at forty for us and our revered rock musicians. Was it possible to be a forty-year-old rock star? But life goes on and new musical directions were not to be denied. The power ballad and anything covered in glitter became de *rigueur*. Men started wearing more make-up than women, shoulder pads were a must and big hair – now directed upwards into artificial feats of topiary – replaced the groomed caveman style that had been the rock musician's badge of honour for so long.

I scoffed at all this, but I now look back on the eighties with a nostalgic smile. That's the music, you understand, not the fashion. I never did shoulder pads because they made me look neanderthal, and I thought glitter looked better on a Christmas tree. Hair? I gave up on that years ago!

This was the start of a period that threatened the dominance of the LP as the prime currency of the music industry. For some years music had been available via other mediums. Firstly there was the eight-track stereo, about as much use as an ashtray on a Harley Davidson, and secondly came the cassette tape. Both had the advantage of allowing listeners to transfer their favourite sounds to private means of transport, but both technologies lacked permanence and reliability. How many times have you seen wispy threads of glossy brown tape glistening in roadside hedges having been hurled from a passing car by a frustrated motorist?

LPs also have their frailties, but they are a more tactile and pleasing thing. They also have the advantage of proportion: their twelve-inch format facilitates artwork, and their dimension makes it possible to read the sleeve notes. With cassettes, the same information came in the form of a tiny, folded paper that required a magnifying glass.

All – or very nearly all of this – was soon brushed aside by the video, followed by the compact disc and then the digital video disc. It was really infuriating, as if the industry was purposely trying to screw us by continually changing the product and the means to play it in a calculated act of exploitation and commercialism.

Towards the end of the decade, CDs started to outsell vinyl records and the prophets suggested it was the death of the twelve-inch medium. Happily, they've been proven wrong; twenty years later, vinyl is staging something of a revival whilst the CD has been usurped by downloading from the internet. Recordings of music no longer form collections treasured and stored in wall units; they are now beamed in from the clouds, not manifested in tangible form and without the benefit of accompanying information. For all they know, today's downloaders could be listening to a ferret strangling a frog, which, on the basis of a lot of recent output, may actually be the case! But let's not fall out over musical preferences. It doesn't matter – no, it *really* doesn't matter. On the evening of the 23rd of October 1984, all such superficiality was put into painfully sharp perspective.

Ethiopia, a country that was no stranger to unrest, drought and famine, was twelve months into another disaster, its problems being compounded by internal politics. The resulting human catastrophe was moving into biblical proportions. The news broadcasts that evening showed a nation abandoned and starving in a desolate, parched landscape that offered them no shelter.

No matter what your musical preferences might have been, we can probably agree that the music business seemed an unlikely place to find someone who was prepared to side-line his career for philanthropic reasons, but that's exactly what Boomtown Rat and, hitherto, loud mouthed gobshite Bob Geldof chose to do. Unlike the vast majority of us coughing up a fiver for Oxfam to ease our consciences, he decided to use his position to make a real difference.

In a remarkably short space of time he assembled an eclectic group of musical chums to record a charity Christmas song. It seems a simple concept but I can't recall it ever having been done before. The resulting single, released on the 29th of November and titled 'Do They Know It's Christmas/Feed The World', sold 3.7 million copies and netted £8million pounds for the Ethiopian Fund.

That was merely the precursor to an even more ambitious fund-raising event. Geldof unveiled plans for two massive concerts at Wembley Stadium and the JFK Stadium, Philadelphia, USA. Live Aid took place on the 13th of July 1985 and was broadcast around the world to an estimated audience of more than two billion people, approximately one third of the world's population.

Throughout the event, the plight of Ethiopia was transferred from the barren wastes of North Africa into our cosy sitting rooms. TV journalist Michael Buerk's commentary described the disaster in all its painful shame. It was a stark wake-up call and, when overdubbed with the Cars song 'Drive', sent a powerful and emotional message to the western world.

I found it disturbing and poignant in equal measures, not so much a wake-up call as a scream to do something to help. It reduced me, and I'm sure many others, to tears. In his introduction to the Live Aid book the much-maligned Mr Geldof wrote:

If there is a meanness, an empty cynicism, a terrifying selfishness and greed in us, then that day, watching that television, dancing in that crowd, playing on that stage, the obverse side of our cruelty was made manifest... We were for a few hours no longer obsessed by ourselves. There was a misery greater than whatever personal nonsense we had to deal with.

There was a desire to help – to do SOMETHING. It was pathetically obvious that in a world of surplus, starvation is the most senseless death of all... What would be possible if we could be like July 13th 1985 all the time?

Live Aid was a triumph of altruism, musical entertainment and logistics and it raised £150m for charity. Simultaneously it sent out a message that, if only for one day, some people in the world cared enough to give their time and their money to support others in distress. What indeed would be possible if we could be like July 13th all the time?

The line-up for Live Aid on each side of the Atlantic was wonderfully varied, and included both young and old musicians. This had me thinking again of the question: is it possible to be a forty-year-old rock star? I considered a selection of those performing on that day – Bob Dylan, Pete Townsend, Eric Clapton, Elton John and Paul McCartney – and discovered their combined years produced an average age of forty-one. They appeared to be doing okay, so there seemed good reason to believe that rock musicians didn't have a sell-by date. Happily this has proved the case as all of those named above continue to entertain us.

19

LEARNING MY TRADE

LANDSCAPE design can be a complicated business that involves working with living material in a dynamic environment exposed to the climate and the demands of a diverse population. In Milton Keynes there was a need to be especially inventive to create a new urban landscape within a rural location. It was as near to a blank sheet as you can get in terms of environmental design. Regard for existing features, especially within the central area, was secondary to the grand design – and the term 'grand design' was not lost on the egos of those architects and engineers who headed up the design team. But as I said before, this was not a great experience for me; my destiny was to be a repairer, a re-builder of our precious landscape and environment.

My new employers at Cleveland County Council had a remit to address the industrial decline that had been damaging the region for many years, and to improve the way in which the area was perceived by others outside the area. In landscape terms, this meant establishing a schedule of damaged sites and giving priority to those close to main transport arteries. My workload included sections of trunk roads adjacent to heavy industrial sites, sections of the River Tees (forming part of an overall plan for the Tees corridor) and strategic plantings within the county.

In addition to our general reclamation activities, our team was seconded to the district councils in Middlesbrough, Hartlepool and

Stockton-on-Tees. Here we helped with housing programmes aimed at lifting the profile of failing estates.

Without doubt there were some successes where lasting improvements were achieved, but there were also occasions when our efforts were subjected to acts of vandalism. At the time I found it very frustrating because we tried to engage with communities through consultation and exhibitions, but such actions are futile if there is no tangible sense of community. Now I'm older (and perhaps wiser) I understand that the environment, whether it is your home or your neighbourhood, is not necessarily top of your priority list, especially in areas where the occupants believe they have been failed by education and political dogma, and where unemployment spans the generations. I have every sympathy for those people. However, I also believe there is a small section of society that chooses to exist outside the community and work ethic, and which thrives on fear and intimidation no matter how much help it may be offered.

I was learning my trade and starting to realise that there is more to landscape architecture than the ability to design in three dimensions using trees, shrubs and elements of built form. It is far more complicated; professionals have to make decisions based on understanding the complexities of specific socio-economic circumstances to ensure that design solutions are both appropriate and cost effective.

Happily, ecologists, landscape architects and urban designers are now involved at the conceptual stages of major schemes; they now work alongside planners, architects and engineers, who have been protective of their status at the head of the table for far too long, often at the expense of good environmental design. It is a problem I've faced continually throughout my career – being confronted with the presupposition that we are in some way lesser beings than our fellow professionals. This curious notion has frequently resulted in landscape architects being late to the party, and having to react to situations that could have been avoided if we'd been consulted earlier. Being adept at camouflaging some hideous design faux pas is not what landscape architecture is about, but it happens. Read on.

In 1986, I started work on the council's proposals for easing congestion problems in Middlesbrough caused by the volume of traffic on the A66. At first I felt flattered at being asked to undertake such a high-profile project, but it didn't take long to realise the proposal under consideration was highly questionable and a potential environmental disaster. The proposed bypass would cut a swathe through the town rather than circumnavigate it. If that were not bad enough, it would also bisect the historic quarter that contained many buildings of architectural significance. Among these was the Royal Exchange, a substantial red-brick building ornamented with stone features, built by Henry Bolckow, the first mayor of Middlesbrough, in 1868 for the trading of iron and steel.

The proposal had been 'bubbling under' for some time. As often happens in areas blighted by indecision, buildings had been abandoned in the expectation of the worst-case scenario. The Royal Exchange was the most notable casualty; by the time the axe fell, its stature within the town was so severely tarnished that it was difficult to defend even by the most ardent of conservationists. I am convinced that today an alternative solution would be found that not only retained The Exchange but all the other Victorian buildings lost to the insensitive eighties' strategy. But in Middlesbrough back in 1986, the damage was already done. I was tasked with looking at ways to mitigate the inevitable consequences of such upheaval. Somebody had to put lipstick on the pig, metaphorically speaking!

A little background might be useful. The proposed road alignment ploughed through the town centre, much of it elevated on a flyover to avoid the local road network and in an attempt not to isolate the northern edge of the town. The Exchange building, like several others to be demolished, was only partially within this corridor so its removal created opportunities for new civic spaces next to the flyover. A poor consolation, but at least it provided an opportunity to add something to a town centre that was sadly lacking in such spaces at the time. So it was that Exchange Square was born.

By the time I started work on the project, my colleague in the conservation department had already resigned himself to the nightmare of losing several prime buildings. I was anxious that our proposals should reflect the area's historical significance in some way and there was a general agreement that the space needed a meaningful focal point. Initially, my ideas were over-elaborate, a trap that is easy to fall into when you're working on high-profile locations.

The breakthrough came when I was chatting with my colleague over a cup of coffee. He reminded me about the sculpture of Henry Bolckow that had been moved to Albert Park from its earlier position next to the Exchange because of traffic congestion problems back in the 1920s. That was it! The statue would provide the ideal focal point, and we even had history on our side to justify its return to the town centre.

It took a little while to win over the doubters but, having done so, the bronze sculpture and its plinth were dismantled, transported on a low-loader and re-erected in Exchange Square. It immediately looked in harmony with its new surroundings, far better than in the park where it had never been intended to stand.

Occasionally I find myself back in the square and remain reasonably satisfied with my handiwork. In the series of books *Britain In Old Photographs* (Middlesbrough Past And Present) Paul Menzies wrote:

Despite its proximity to the A66, Exchange Square (as it is now renamed) is an elegant tree-lined area, once again under the scrutiny of Henry Bolckow, whose statue stands in its midst.

I think Mr Menzies is being kind; whilst the square has succeeded reasonably well aesthetically, it has been something of a disappointment because as a whole the project failed to unlock its potential to become a major civic space. We hoped that its creation would breathe new life into this rather neglected part of the town and enhance the marketability of surrounding buildings, particularly the elegant, curved terrace at its northern edge. Sadly this has not happened, though this was probably always going to be a bit optimistic in a town that had faced fifty years of depression and neglect.

Seriously overshadowed by the new elevated A66, Exchange Square has never become the busy civic space we hoped for. It only comes alive at weekends when the pub beneath the arches of the flyover occasionally spills out a little of its merriment. Sometimes, no matter how hard you try, there's only so much lipstick you can put on a pig.

⊙⊙⊙

Despite the ups and downs, I loved my job. It was incredibly satisfying to be involved in restoring derelict landscapes that had suffered the ravages of heavy, polluting industries, to plant sapling trees and to see healthy young woodlands where previously there was rubble, twisted metal and desolation.

During the last quarter of the century there have been many environmental improvements to the Teesside area and I'm proud to have played a small part as a team member at Cleveland County from 1982 to 1989. Our team played a huge part in restoring a landscape that had suffered a century of exploitation and was in serious decline. Driving around the area today there is plenty of evidence of the hard work that was put in – and the Council's achievements were all the more remarkable given the government's antipathy towards our northern cities.

20

MAMAS AND PAPAS

IN March 1986 I became the proud father of a beautiful daughter who changed my life for the better and for ever.

It's strange: we all know what is going to happen, yet somehow we're never quite prepared for the emotion that comes with having a child. By the time my wife and I entered the maternity suite, I was reaching the stage where dads-to-be become jabbering useless appendages as the mums-to-be shoulder all the pain and responsibility.

I'm amazed how women have the fortitude to carry a child for nine months and cope with giving birth. I offer a big thank you to you all for putting yourselves through the agony and miracle of childbirth. It seems you have God to thank for all the pain; in Genesis chapter 3, verse 16, He tells Eve (in what I would suggest was one of his less benevolent moments): *I will make your pains in childbearing very severe; with painful labour you will give birth to children. Your desire will be for your husband and he will rule over you.*

I reckon that's a bit much for scrumping an apple!

We embarked on that road of uncertainty travelled by first-time parents, terrified of doing something wrong and suddenly aware of a huge new responsibility. Now, of course, I know exactly what is involved. To anyone who is thinking of making an amorous move on their beloved, I say take a minute to consider this: what you are about to do could result in sleepless nights, some three years of puke and disgusting nappies, fifteen to twenty years of educational trauma and hormonal tantrums, and a lifetime of worry. And that's if it all goes well!

On the other hand, you will see your child smile for the first time, walk for the first time, develop their own personality and quite possibly achieve more in life than you ever managed.

⊙ ⊙ ⊙

That same year, I was concerned about the world into which my daughter had just arrived. Within six weeks of her birth, the nuclear power station at Chernobyl in Ukraine suffered a massive explosion. It is estimated that the radioactive fallout was one hundred times greater than the bombs dropped on Nagasaki and Hiroshima. In the days and weeks that followed, this fallout drifted across pretty much the entire European continent, including Britain.

The immediate death toll was recorded as thirty-one but there have been 4,000 cancer-related deaths attributed to the incident. Reports by authoritative scientific bodies predict cancer-related deaths could, over a given period of time, be as many as 50–60,000 more than what might be considered the average statistic.

Bob Dylan has insisted that 'A Hard Rain's a-Gonna Fall'; written in 1963, is not about atomic fallout. That's as may be, but in the week after Chernobyl 'hard rain' was falling in Wales, the Lake District, Western Scotland and the Highlands, contaminating grassland and the farm produce dependent upon it. Initially around 9,000 farms were affected; a few locations still had restrictions on stock movements into the new millennium.

The same year, concern grew regarding the deadly HIV/AIDS virus. Until now it had been a problem most commonly associated firstly with Africa and then the more sexually promiscuous in our own population. Now it was emerging in more conservative sections of society. As part of an awareness campaign, the government commissioned a TV information film; its most memorable image was a tombstone with

AIDS etched across it and the shadowy figure of the grim reaper. It was all very scary stuff.

With radioactive rain falling just down the road in the Lake District and the prospect of a deadly virus growing within our society, I wondered about the world my daughter would inherit. Thirty years later, I'm still aghast at the irresponsibility of man toward his environment and life itself.

⊙⊙⊙

Notwithstanding disease, pestilence and nuclear rain, Christmas 1986 was a wonderful time as we celebrated our first Christmas as a family. It was also a time to take stock, to start looking forward. How could I further my career and, more importantly, guarantee the wellbeing of my family?

Much as I was enjoying my working life with the council, there was an elephant in the room that could not be ignored. Several of my colleagues and I were at the same stage in our careers, all with similar aspirations in terms of professional status and salary. With little or no possibility of promotion at the council, the break-up of our team was inevitable.

My departure occurred a year later when I spotted a job opportunity with a private practice established and run by a college contemporary of mine who was now based in Portsmouth. He planned to expand the business and wanted someone to open an office in Birmingham. After a brief discussion in a Pizza Hut just outside Birmingham the deal was done. I would head up the company's new office but in Middlesbrough rather than Birmingham, where we believed there were similar business opportunities to be found.

A few months later I said goodbye to my colleagues at Cleveland Council and moved a few hundred yards down the road to a new office in Broadcasting House. I had a desk, a chair, a filing cabinet and a drawing board – and I was absolutely terrified.

It was the start of a new chapter in my professional life as the security and comfort of local government were replaced by the uncertainties of the private sector. The next twenty years proved to be a roller-coaster of optimism, regrets, exhilaration and pain. Safe, dependable old John had thrown away the script and there was no going back.

It began badly. Little more than twelve months after rejecting the relative safety of local government, I felt the full force of a ruthless and unforgiving private sector. My MD phoned me to say the company was experiencing financial problems and he was intending to pull the plug before the situation became too damaging. It was a great shock, but his foresight in taking this difficult decision at least offered a parachute by way of a pay cheque equal to about ninety percent of my normal monthly wage.

I thought I would be panic-stricken and fretful, but I was actually very calm and uncharacteristically confident that something would turn up. My confidence was not misplaced; within days I was asked to call in at an architectural practice in Middlesbrough for which I was preparing designs for a small housing scheme. After a brief chat, the deed was done. I closed the door for the last time on my little office in Broadcasting House where I'd spent a fairly lonely year, and joined my new colleagues for the next phase of my career.

Having weathered the storm of possible unemployment, we turned our thoughts to our daughter's education and the best place for her to spend those important school years. These decisions are tougher today than they were for our parents. Above all, you want your child to be happy.

With our future looking more assured, in November 1990 we decided to move to Borrowby, about five miles south east of Northallerton. Our daughter started her junior education at the village school a few hundred yards from our new home. It was a new school building beside its Victorian predecessor (which had been turned into a pair of houses). I couldn't help reflecting on how the community had changed in that time span. Most of the kids attending the Victorian school were from farming families, but growing crops and rearing livestock had become heavily mechanised businesses managed by a much-reduced workforce. As a result, quaint little villages like Borrowby have become dormitories for office workers commuting to towns far afield – in this case Middlesbrough and York. I was one of these commuters.

The school pick-up was the time to see this diversity, exemplified by the mix of vehicles that arrived at the school gates. Before they could bundle their precious little packages into Chelsea Tractor or mud-spattered Defender (or in my case a Renault 5), there was that awful waiting period when all the latest gossip was exchanged. I loved being able to walk my daughter to school and pick her up, but school-gate chit-chat made me very uncomfortable.

Worst of all was the arrival of the 'momager', the pushy and insanely ambitious mum. I believe there is at least one at every school gate in every town or village in every county the length and breadth of the land. If you have kids of your own, I'm sure you've encountered them. This mum can't resist telling you that her little Isolde (aged six) is speaking fluent Latin and Mandarin, and is totally absorbed with nuclear physics when she's not riding her pony, though she might have to give that up because she's in training with the British skiing team for the next winter Olympics. We've planned Roedean for Isolde, then Oxford ... obviously.

Why do these people inflict so much pressure on their kids? It seems, the age of innocence is becoming ever shorter, so it should be our priority to see that it is a time that is happy and carefree. Let them have fun and do stupid, nonsensical things for a while. There will still be plenty of aggravation, frustration and anxiety when they are grown up, so why burden them so soon?

21

THE THATCHER LEGACY

I have devoted an entire chapter to Margaret Thatcher because I believe she changed our society more than any other person during my lifetime.

In 1979, Britain was a rather troubled country. In her first seemingly impromptu (but no doubt well-rehearsed) speech, the newly elected leader quoted St Francis of Assisi, saying:

'Where there is discord, may we bring harmony. Where there is error, may we bring truth, Where there is doubt, may we bring faith. And where there is despair, may we bring hope'.

The new, self-styled St Francis was quickly put to the test when unrest spilled onto the streets of Toxteth, Liverpool. In fairness, Thatcher's government cannot be held responsible for Toxteth; it had been in decline for some time and had one of the highest unemployment rates in the UK. The economic recession was hitting Liverpool very hard, especially in the dockland area where traditional waterfront jobs were being lost to containerisation. Add to this a growing unrest brought about by heavy-handed policing of the black community and you had a riot waiting to happen. Sure enough, on the 3rd of July the lid well and truly came off.

Thatcher's response was to despatch her trusty lieutenant (and later her political assassin) Michael Heseltine to solve this complex problem. Of the measures suggested to deal with it, the most unlikely but probably best remembered was the proposal for a garden festival on derelict land beside the Mersey. As a tool to deal with deeply rooted cultural and socio-economic problems, it was a lame and ineffective response to a serious problem.

Liverpool, like many other industrial towns and cities, was perceived as a Tory-free zone and therefore of no value to the preservation of Thatcher's government. In recent years, documents have been released that give an insight into how the Home Secretary, the late Lord Howe, viewed the problems. He described the city of Liverpool as: *a concentration of hopelessness, largely self-inflicted with its record of industrial strife.* He warned Mrs Thatcher:

...not to commit scarce resources to Liverpool ...we do not want to find ourselves concentrating all the limited cash that may have to be made available into Liverpool and having nothing left for possibly more promising areas such as the West Midlands or, even, the North East... I cannot help feeling that the option of managed decline is one which we should not forget altogether.

Whilst it was the industrial towns that were feeling more pain than most, the nation as a whole was in serious economic decline. Clearly something had to change in order to steady the ship and fill the depleted coffers of HM Treasury. Thatcher's solution was a mega car-boot sale.

First up was an instruction to local authorities to sell off their stocks of council houses, or at least offer them for sale to their tenants. It was an idea that had been flirted with over many years by both Labour and Conservative administrations but never acted upon, but in 1980 'the right to buy' was a substantial part of a new housing act. At the time it seemed perfectly reasonable; I can hardly criticise it, given that my parents were amongst the first to take advantage of it. There was, however, a major downside that meant that the winners back in the 1980s would be matched by as many – and more – losers thirty years down the line.

Next came the bargain-basement sale of the nation's public utilities (or the 'family silver' as they became known). One by one, electricity, telephone, water and gas were privatised. The sales were promoted to attract the attention of the average man in the street, or at least those with some spare cash. British Gas used TV advertising and a colloquial catchphrase, 'Tell Sid', the inference being that you – yes, even you – could make a fast buck by buying a few shares. It worked politically, but again there were long-term ramifications.

These were the tactics of a leader attempting to refashion the working class. In doing so, she gave credence to greed and applauded wealth creation for individuals by any means, regardless of the consequences it might have for others. Do you recall Harry Enfield's 'loads-a-money' character? From spiv to banker everyone seemed to be on the make, spawning a tide of binge consumerism, a phenomenon that continues to this day.

The political theory behind this was that society's preoccupation with acquiring consumer goods and services would sustain the economy. It glossed over the damage inflicted on the environmental resource base so comprehensively that people didn't even realise there was a problem. Jonathan Porritt, the renowned environmentalist, put it very much into perspective when he stated:

Many ideas have struggled over the centuries to dominate the planet. Fascism. Communism. Democracy. Religion. But only one has achieved total supremacy. Its compulsive attractions rob its followers of reason and good sense. It has created unsustainable inequalities and threatened to tear apart the very fabric of society. More powerful than any religion, it has reached into every corner of the globe. It is consumerism.

At the 1980 Conservative Party Conference, Thatcher defended her controversial plans to liberalise employment, taunting her doubters with the now familiar phrase, *'You turn (U-turn) if you want to, the lady's not for turning.'* It was a move that gave credence to globalisation, the process of worldwide interaction and integration between people, companies and governments.

Opinions on the value of globalisation differ greatly. Some would argue that it keeps prices low for western consumers whilst maximising income to company shareholders – but how does it achieve this? This is where I have a problem. It seems that we consumers often reap the benefits by allowing others elsewhere in the world to work in conditions akin to slavery and by abdicating our responsibility on a whole raft of environmental issues. Electrical goods and the fashion industry appear to be two of the worst offenders.

Having said that, I confess that economics are an anathema to me so I shall draw on the words of one of our most celebrated economists, John Maynard Keynes:

'I sympathise with those who would minimize rather than those who would maximize, economic enlargement among nations. Ideas, knowledge, science, hospitality, travel ... these are the things which should of their nature be international. But let goods be home spun whenever it is reasonably and conveniently possible, and, above all let finance be primarily national.'

The rush to embrace globalisation has changed the face of industrial Britain. Companies we once thought of as the bedrock of UK manufacturing have been lost to foreign owners. Rolls Royce is one example: the motor manufacturing manifestation of the brand, once the hallmark of quality within the British car industry, is now owned by BMW, the company that manufactured aircraft engines for the Luftwaffe during WW2.

There can be no more telling example of this phenomena than HP sauce, the nation's number-one choice to complement a full-English breakfast. Its logo depicts Big Ben and the Houses of Parliament but it's about as British as Kentucky Fried Chicken and Gouda. It was bought in 2006 by Heinz, who promptly closed the Birmingham factory and transferred production to the Netherlands with the loss of more than 120 jobs. This act so infuriated constituency MP Khalid Mahmood that he raised the issue in the House of Commons and brandished a bottle of HP sauce in protest against Heinz's actions.

Under Thatcher, British industry was sold out. The government's disregard for manufacturing has allowed hostile takeovers where shareholders benefit and employees' job security is put at risk. I think that far too many companies have been sacrificed to foreign competitors, leading to profits going abroad to foreign economies. I'm left wondering if the free-market system of boardrooms and shareholders will ever deliver a healthy, symbiotic relationship between our captains of industry and those who actually keep the wheels turning.

⊙⊙⊙

In the spring of 1984, Thatcher was very much in the ascendancy. The short-term benefits of her economic policies were attracting the support of middle England. Having dealt with the Falklands and the Gulf War, she turned her attention to demolishing the trade-union movement. Top of her list was Arthur Scargill, head of the National Union of Mineworkers (NUM), and to this end she appointed Ian MacGregor as her chief executioner.

Times were changing and the mining industry could not be exempt from this process, but the vitriolic attack directed at the mining community was shocking. These were communities on which the nation had built its wealth over many years and they didn't warrant such heavy-handed treatment.

Clearly both parties in this conflict had their own personal crusades. Thatcher wanted to destroy the union movement, come what may, and Scargill adopted an intractable position that was untenable in a rapidly changing world.

It was the beginning of the end for deep-shaft mining in the UK – which, strangely enough, was the one thing Scargill anticipated correctly. He had long claimed that MacGregor intended to close more than seventy collieries, an accusation that was vehemently denied but which proved to be the case. Scargill might have gained more traction had such information been available at the time but, in a nation that for many years had been hamstrung by union despots, his attempts to win over 'hearts and minds' were generally greeted with antipathy.

Thatcher gained politically from this and went on to treat the trade-union movement with vengeful contempt and a malevolence that left me, a relative newcomer to the heartland of industrial, socialist Britain feeling like a stranger at a wake.

She could afford to bash the unions because there were no votes to be lost there, but she needed to make some attempt to arrest the decline in the northern cities where old-established industries were coming under threat.

To this end, she commissioned a number of development corporations in Merseyside, Teesside and Tyne and Wear but, unlike the corporations that had existed before (and of which I had some experience), these were led by the private sector. I was working in Middlesbrough throughout most of the life of the Teesside Corporation, and I can honestly say it was of very little benefit for the local community. Some industrial wilderness was erased and there were new projects, but these were generally designed and implemented without considering local needs and by absentee companies and design teams.

The architectural practice I was working for had little opportunity to bid for work. When we did seize the chance to enter, prepare plans for, and eventually win a corporation-run design competition, the promise of fulfilling what would have been a lucrative commission was taken from us. The work was mysteriously awarded to a practice in Cheshire amidst allegations of cronyism and self-interest within the corporation.

I think that Thatcher's intentions for these areas came with an ulterior motive; she would have done them a better service if she had funded the local councils to carry out the improvements *they* wished to achieve so they were more cost effective and accountable to the local communities. In reality, she was doing little more than a PR job on regions blighted by economic, environmental and social problems.

Eventually her autocratic style started to disenfranchise a wider audience. Just ten years after the Toxteth riots, unrest boiled over on our streets again – but not in a northern city.

On the 31st March 1990, Central London was the venue for a major demonstration. Thatcher's plans to replace the old domestic rates system was interpreted by a whole swathe of society as an opportunity for extortion on a grand scale. The new method, then referred to as the poll tax, was thought to favour the wealthy at the expense of lower-income families, which it clearly did. The Prime Minister insisted on sticking to her guns, but her doggedness signalled the beginning of the end. She had become irretrievably unpopular with the electorate, a situation that hastened her demise as PM when she was dumped by her former colleagues and supporters.

⊙⊙⊙

So what do we make of Thatcher and the legacy of Thatcherism? She came to power at a difficult time. The economy was in deep decline. The decline of coal mining was inevitable, and in some sectors the industrial base was still dogged by union radicals. To some she turned the nation around, but by others she is perceived as the force that set in motion attitudes in society that have led to division, greed and a lack of compassion.

She may have brought about an improvement to the economy but I remain troubled by her methods, which I believe had a profound impact on our society, little of which has been for good.

Fundamental to her short-term economic revival was winning over working/middle England. She achieved this with the sale of council houses and by encouraging people to become shareholders, a ploy that may have worked as a political tactic but has proved spectacularly damaging on two counts. Firstly, when sanctioning the sale of council houses Thatcher prevented those same councils from replenishing their housing stock and significantly diminished the bank of social housing. This has developed into a serious national problem, aided and abetted by subsequent governments that have failed to address it. Secondly, we were led to believe that the sell-off of state-owned services would stimulate competition and lead to more competitive pricing. That hasn't been the case. The vast majority of shares in privatised companies

126

ended up in the hands of large city conglomerates, many of which are not British. In effect, we have gone from publicly-owned monopolies to a cartel of companies. Companies have become empowered to make vast profit irrespective of customer service and with no duty of care to the environment. The quality of our environment should never have been entrusted to the free market.

And what of Thatcher's long-term economic plan? It is often referred to as the 'trickle-down' theory, whereby the wealthy are given tax breaks so they can stimulate the economy through their increased ability to spend. In doing so, they will supposedly expand business and manufacturing and, ultimately, the wage packets of the less fortunate. But business, especially in manufacturing, was betrayed by Thatcher; thousands of jobs were lost, particularly in industrial towns in the North and Midlands, in large-scale closures that have impaired local economies and eroded our manufacturing base. This process was also fuelled by the sale of companies to organisations outside the UK and by the systematic destruction of the unions to such an extent that they are still regarded with suspicion, despite a significant degradation of worker's rights and conditions most notably in the retail and leisure sectors.

The business/manufacturing environment has become more difficult, a situation further compounded by the financial sector. In harnessing and exploiting the worst excesses of Thatcherism, it was empowered to gamble in the markets to create wealth for shareholders and high fliers. The business model that was for so long the mainstay of industry and employment within the UK has largely been abandoned. The nation's risk takers and entrepreneurs, whose creative talents and invention have traditionally underpinned the nation's manufacturing, now struggle to get investment.

Even if she didn't single-handedly change us from a 'we' to an 'I' society, Thatcher stoked a fire that has burned out of control ever since. She was widely reported as saying '*there is no such thing as society*'. In fairness, this comment was taken out of context, but by her actions and policies she appeared to be hell-bent on creating a nation of haves and have nots, destroying much of our industry and widening the division between the north and south. Indeed, the north/south divide seems destined never to be addressed. In recent years it has been exacerbated by further Thatcherite Tory governments intent on growing the London economy to the detriment of other regions.

I believe that the bias towards London and the service industry is even more extreme than it was. Funding for infrastructure and transport in the capital runs into hundreds of billions of pounds. In 2015, London First, supposedly a not-for-profit advocacy but in fact representing the interests of hundreds of London-based businesses, presented a paper, *London's Infrastructure – Investing For Growth*, which stated:

London's success is of benefit to the UK at large... Construction and infrastructure spent on London projects directly benefits many parts of the rest of the country.

I'm not sure how well that claim plays out on the back streets of Toxteth. And the name, London First, does rather say it all!

With bankers earning millions for themselves irrespective of performance, the upper echelons of middle England being empowered to feed off the property market, and a growing section of society made homeless and driven to dependency on food banks and handouts, it appears that the 'trickle down' hasn't trickled down very far. The reality is more Voltairian philosophy than Thatcherite policy; as Voltaire said: '*The comfort of the rich depends upon an abundant supply of the poor.*' Sadly, much of society seems to have become blind (or at least resigned) to this situation, preferring to immerse itself in unsustainable consumerism and culturally impoverished distractions fuelled by TV ads that promote avarice and gambling, whilst espousing the virtues of money lenders, the banks having long since abdicated such services.

Intentionally or not, Thatcher created a fractured nation of winners and losers. I'm not sure St Francis of Assisi would have been particularly impressed by her misappropriation of his well-meaning and comforting words.

Having said that, it would be remiss of me not to mention the way she resolutely protected the nation on the international scene.

Diplomatically, and at times of conflict, she was never found wanting. She always defended the best interests of Britain as she saw them, often to the discomfort and displeasure of our European colleagues. In this respect she was arguably our best leader since Churchill.

'Confrontational' is a fair way of describing her method of governing. It served her well in conflict abroad in the Falklands and the Middle East, but often delivered unrest onto the streets of her own country. The greed and consumerism promoted by her divisive policies has become an abiding legacy within our society some twenty years after her departure from government.

It was a term of office that initiated a sea change in the way we worked and lived, bringing with it a less cohesive society exemplified in 1985 by singer/songwriter Billy Bragg. His stark song 'Between The Wars' was a cry for faith and compassion over greed and indifference.

But hang on a minute, I hear you say. Just a few pages back you were making the case for having more women in positions of authority, and you can't get a more powerful position than Prime Minister. You are correct in pointing this out – I just didn't count on the Iron Lady of Assisi – sorry, Grantham!

22

FAITH, HOPE AND CALAMITY

THE transition of the 1980s to the 1990s was a reasonably happy time, or at least acceptably uneventful. My life seemed to be on an even keel. I had recovered from the trauma of redundancy and was now settling into family life.

There were reasons to be cheerful elsewhere in the world. Earlier I reflected upon the 1961 Cuban crisis. Happily a nuclear situation was averted then, but later that same year events in Berlin saw the temperature of the Cold War grow ever more icy when the East German authorities partitioned the city. The Berlin Wall was a deterrent to stop, as they saw it, disenfranchised East Germans fleeing their oppressors for a better life in the West. Its construction split friends and family groups, some of whom suddenly found themselves estranged from loved ones and people they had grown up with.

During the years of partition, many people attempted to circumnavigate the barbed wire fences that preceded the wall and 136 lost their lives trying to do so. But by the autumn of 1989 there was a palpable thaw in the air, largely brought about by a new Russian leader, Mikhail Gorbachev. His programme of *Glasnost* (openness) allowed more freedom to the Soviet States, eventually leading to their independence and self-determination. In Berlin he effectively emasculated the East German regime; when crowds gathered at the wall, symbolically chipping away the massive structure, the military authorities were powerless to react. Germany was reunified.

To my mind, Gorbachev was an extraordinary man and his leadership transformed the outdated regimes of the old Soviet Union. Through his negotiations with US president, Ronald Reagan, he brought about change that significantly eased tensions between the East and West. He went on to win a Nobel Peace Prize before being unceremoniously and scandalously ousted by Boris Yeltsin, who capitalised on the changes initiated by Gorbachev.

Yeltsin, it seems, was perceived as being more a man of the people, but he proved to be an inferior leader and ended up a figure of ridicule. Sadly, however, the damage was done, not just for Russia but the world.

Whilst the good burghers of Germany immersed themselves in the warm afterglow of unification, the start of the new decade saw another nation on another continent take a massive step forward along its evolutionary path by ridding itself of a governing regime that ruled by racial and ethnic division. Would it now be possible for black families to live alongside white in a truly integrated African society?

In February 1990, F.W. de Klerk, Prime Minister of South Africa, assisted by the imprisoned civil rights leader Nelson Mandela, abolished the regulations that criminalised all political opposition groups. In doing so, they quelled mounting unrest and effectively brought an end to the regime of apartheid that had been ruthlessly and brutally administered by the white minority ruling party for the best part of fifty years. Nelson Mandela, having served twenty-seven years in prison for opposing white government rule, was released. This quote says much about the great man.

To be free is not merely to cast off one's chains, but to live in a way that respects and enhances the freedom of others.

Mandela and de Klerk were awarded Nobel Peace Prizes, and Mandela eventually became the nation's first black president.

As East/West relations improved significantly and South Africa began the process of building a more integrated society, tensions were mounting elsewhere in the world. The next few years were turbulent, with troubles in both the Balkans and the Middle East.

In August 1990 Iraq invaded and then occupied Kuwait, legitimising its actions through an oil-drilling dispute, though arguably Iraq wanted to boost its ailing economy that had been weakened by an eight-year conflict with neighbouring Iran. On the 17th of January 1991, coalition forces (including thirty-four nations from all four corners of the world) carried out air strikes on strategic targets.

Code-named 'Desert Storm' and led by the US, the onslaught was designed to weaken Iraq's occupying forces prior to a full military invasion. It was as devastating as it was decisive, paving the way for a ground assault that began on the 24th of February, and which overwhelmed the Iraqi forces in less than four days. Job done – or was it? Sure, Kuwait had been liberated but, as is so often the case following such interventions, it left behind another set of problems. In this case, there was a beleaguered Iraqi nation with a defeated – but not deposed – dictator still at its head. Saddam Hussain would continue his ruthless tyranny over the nation for several more years.

I guess it was easy to understand the cause and effect of this war: one nation was invaded by a neighbouring aggressor, therefore others (via the auspices of many nations united in coalition) rushed to its assistance. Oh yes – and to protect their oil interests. But I find what happened in Yugoslavia some four months later confusing and disturbing to this very day. To me, it defied all logic.

Until 1991, Yugoslavia was a country I knew very little about other than it being one of the countries that made up the eastern block of Europe. It was notionally communist and led by that rarest of species, a firm but relatively fair dictator, Marshal Tito. Apart from that, I knew very little about the place.

Tito seemed to be well-regarded by both parties to the Cold War, thereby achieving stability within and respect from without his nation, a status it enjoyed until his death in 1980. It was only then that the true identity and make up of the population appeared – and for all the wrong reasons.

Growing unrest, stoked by religious and ethnic prejudice, eventually boiled over in the summer of 1991 when the Serbian sector attempted to impose its dominance upon the other constituent federal states. This action led people, who were once neighbours, friends and family living in relative harmony, to suddenly take up arms against each other.

I had always thought of Europe as a relatively civilised place where the disasters and tragedies of two world wars were now drifting gently into the annals of history. I was clearly mistaken. For the next ten years there were reports of horrific atrocities, the like of which I thought could never happen on European soil. They gave rise to a new and horrific expression, 'ethnic cleansing'. It seemed that, as in Nazi Germany some fifty years earlier, respect and tolerance had no place in Yugoslavia.

No sooner had the fires of apartheid in South Africa been stamped out than one of its fellow nations, Rwanda, embarked on a bloody civil war fuelled by long-standing tribal rivalry. The genocide that ensued lasted only one hundred days, from the 7the of April to mid-July 1994, but more than 800,000 Tutsis were murdered, mostly by Hutus.

Whether it was Rwanda, the Balkans or Vietnam, it seemed that geography and culture were irrelevant. Something dangerous and irrational lurks deep within the brain of man, be they black, white or brown, Christian, Muslim, Buddhist, Jew, that seems to be capable of overcoming decency and fellowship and provoking levels of aggression and brutality that defy all understanding. It is difficult not to think that maybe the world – and I hesitate to use the word civilisation – is destined to fall foul of such atrocities in perpetuity. Or do you think there may still be hope for us all?

23

A BIG MISTAKE

IT is pretty much impossible to relate our mundane lives to the terrors I've just described, but life as *we* know it goes on. For me, that meant recovering from the false dawn that had been my preliminary sortie into the private sector. Fortunately, professional and financial disaster had been averted, and I'd learned some useful lessons. Things were back on track: we had an income; mortgage payments were met, and all was well with my little corner of the world.

My new employer in Middlesbrough also had offices in Edinburgh and Perth. It was through my colleagues north of the border that I was introduced to a company whose patronage would become very important to me over the next few years. This was Safeway, which at the time was constructing many new stores to keep pace with their competitors who had similar expansionist ideas.

The Perth office was working on two new supermarkets in Perth itself and Stevenston on the Ayrshire coast and I was brought in to prepare landscape designs for both projects. It wasn't the most glamorous of work but it all helped, especially when I was under some pressure to prove my worth as the only landscape architect within the company. These commissions turned out pretty well. Before they were complete, I was summoned to Safeway HQ at Bellshill, near Glasgow, for briefings on further projects where I would be working with other architectural practices.

Prompted by fierce competition, new stores were being commissioned at a startling rate. I was soon travelling to sites across Scotland and the north of England, from Fort William to Darlington, and East Kilbride to Berwick-upon-Tweed. My claim for a company car gained momentum with every train ticket I bought or car I hired.

I quite enjoyed the travelling. I especially remember one early morning start heading out to Fort William. The last section of the journey, across Rannoch Moor and down through Glencoe, was usually steeped in mist and rain and the presence of its awful history, but on this occasion I was greeted by a clear, fresh, autumnal morning. I parked the car in a layby and looked across at the steep mountainside adorned with the butter-yellow foliage of larch and birch trees, above them the peaks capped with the first snows and above those the clearest of blue skies. It was a perfect landscape and I remember thinking that it would be hard to beat anywhere in the world. We have so much to be thankful for in our small yet diverse islands.

Back in the office there was a new issue to consider. A London company wanted to take us over, together with several others including a York-based practice, in an attempt to establish themselves as a national business. It was a market-listed company noted for undertaking very substantial commissions, including the redevelopment of Terminal 3 at Heathrow. I thought it would be a positive step forward; it appeared to give access to a wider client base and would provide a degree of stability during the inevitable times when work was slow or hard to find. Unfortunately, my assessment was stupendously wrong.

It soon looked like a total mismatch. Our new masters were indifferent to our provincial ways and had no interest in our *modus operandi*, other than bequeathing their name, which actually helped no one. We were suddenly regarded with suspicion where before we had been perceived as a well-established, reliable business within the Teesside area. While we ploughed our parochial furrow, they continued to pursue the 'big one'. Unfortunately the economy was heading into recession once again and major design projects, for so long the life blood of our parent company, were becoming few and far between.

Something had to give and it did – big time! When the shit hit the fan in London, it spattered over us via plummeting share values. I had never stopped to consider the pitfalls of being a publicly listed company. Had I done so, I might have been less enthusiastic about the takeover, but I'd assumed (against my usual instincts) that bigger was better.

We struggled on despite the difficult economic climate. As things turned out, for a while I was the chief beneficiary of our new status, and I was called in to work with our Belfast office on a substantial retail development in Derry. A few months earlier the prospect of making regular visits to these cities would have scared the bejesus out of me, since they were the two most volatile towns during the sectarian unrest. Happily for the good people of Northern Ireland – and fortunately for me – my activities took place during a period of calm as the various factions had just made a declaration of peace.

So I found myself at stupid o'clock in the morning at Teesside Airport, waiting for a flight into Belfast City and my first briefing. The little plane sped down the runway and launched itself steeply away from grey Teesside, quickly topping the mountains and valleys of the Lake District before passing over the coast. Within the hour we were looking down across the Isle of Man and making our descent toward Belfast Loch guided by the giant gantries of Harland and Wolff ship builders of the *Titanic*, another monument to our once illustrious industrial past.

It was a journey I made several times in the coming months, usually without incident except for one notable occasion. I was sitting in the terminal at Teesside Airport just after the early morning 'red-eye' flight to London had emptied the concourse of passengers when a call went out for me. I went to the enquiries office where I was told that the plane was late coming up from Leeds. At that point, I deduced that I was the only passenger! A little while earlier I could have counted the number of flights I'd made on one hand; now I had my own personal executive plane!

The project became known as Foyleside because it was close to the banks of the River Foyle and a mere stone's throw from the infamous Bogside, where the gable ends of houses have been adorned with sectarian art work. Our project was a substantial piece of urban redevelopment, replacing a rather tired and nondescript section of the old city centre with a multi-level shopping complex and car park separated by a proposed new civic space. That is where I came in.

It was a difficult and demanding project, similar in some ways to the Royal Exchange site in Middlesbrough. This was also to be primarily a town-centre pedestrian area but it was complicated by a bus route that needed to have as little visual impact as possible. It was a bit tricky, but I think it turned out okay.

The centre had been open for only a few months when I received copy of a letter from a senior officer at the DOE (Northern Ireland), which read: *I was attending a meeting in the city yesterday and had an opportunity to look around the Foyleside development. Many congratulations on the design and implementation of such an impressive scheme.*

After all this rushing about, I was eventually rewarded with a company car. Our MD in Middlesbrough decided to retire so I was given his ageing Renault 25. As I was used to driving Minis, Metros and Renault 5s it was something of a challenge, not least because it was an automatic and had the turning circle of the *QE2*. And as for the seats – I felt like I was driving around in Barker and Stonehouse's shop window! Sadly, the gearbox gave up within a matter of months and it was written off.

I then received another hand-me-down in the form of a Peugeot 404 with 135,000 miles on the clock, an inside head lining that appeared to be growing mushrooms and a body shell that was gently composting. Suffice to say, my dreams of having a company car were very short lived.

By the beginning of 1995 the company was looking decidedly shaky. The workload had diminished significantly, so some pruning seemed inevitable. Following the departure of our MD, we became subordinate to, and under the management of, the York office. It was no great surprise when the hatchet eventually fell on Middlesbrough. For a while I felt sure I would transfer to York, given that I was the only landscape architect within the group, and I travelled down to York to discuss the situation with my new boss. We had a brief conversation during which he painted a grim picture of how things were. It was worse than I had expected; massive changes were already afoot.

I'd never envisaged being a freelance consultant but that was effectively what I became the moment I walked out of his office. I tidied things up, took my final salary and drove away in my geriatric Peugeot, a parting gift that formed the centrepiece of a non-existent severance package. As I drove the twenty miles down the A19, there was so much racing through my mind. Had I enough money for my next mortgage payment? And how was I, the world's worst businessman, going to survive on my own?

24

THE CHELSEA FLOWER SHOW

FREELANCE is a strange word. I've just looked it up in my dictionary – you remember dictionaries, those collections of pages we used to look at before we all Googled.

...one of the mercenary knights and men-at-arms who after the Crusades wandered about Europe: an unattached journalist, politician etc,: anyone who works for himself, without an employer.

I rather like the idea of galloping around the countryside on my white charger designing knot gardens for aristocratic ladies. I think I'd have been good at that.

Working from home takes a bit of getting used to. It can be a very lonely place. In my case, I started work in a cold attic office accompanied by an old radio spluttering out hours of Radio 4 and Radio 2. My Radio 1 days had been consigned to history.

For me, the early nineties were a desert of musical mediocrity, save for those who plied their trade under the title of indie (independent). Will someone please explain to me what the hell is hip-hop, teen-pop, g-funk, techno, rave and grunge? Best not. And I don't believe my life will be in any way diminished if I never again hear Shaggy, Bjork, Right Said Fred, Beastie Boys and Wu Tang Clan. Just give me good old Terry Wogan – though in fairness to Mr W, he did introduce new talent into his daily fare of golden oldies, comfortable nostalgia and scurrilous wit.

Radio fatigue apart, the most difficult thing about working from home is being disciplined enough to work regular hours. It's so easy to be tempted away by test matches on the TV or taking time out on a sunny day to do a bit of gardening. Such dalliances can result in burning the midnight oil to catch up, which is not fair to those who live with you. It is likely to disturb them, and excessive late-night shifts tend to turn mild-mannered people like me into grouchy, short-tempered pains in the butt.

You also need to be wary of clients who take advantage of you because they know you can do an all-nighter if necessary to retrieve some internal programming nightmare they could have avoided with a bit of forward planning. They have you by the short and curlies, knowing full well that you can't afford to turn down work or damage the relationship you have painstakingly built up.

There is also the constant nagging in the back of your mind that you'll have to bring out all those little screwed-up bits of paper and organise them for your accountant. Most important of all, you must complete your VAT return as Mr VAT doesn't like being messed around.

The number one priority is earning enough money to pay the mortgage and put food on the table for your family. It is at times when things go pear-shaped with cash flow, as they sometimes do, that you feel most vulnerable and exposed. Like Mr VAT man, Messrs Lloyd, Barclay and Halifax etc. can go apoplectic at the mention of words like 'time' and 'extensions thereof'. Somehow they don't seem to see the injustice in taking five days to clear a cheque while at the same time charging you for being one day overdrawn, the cheque in question being the one you waited six weeks for from some multi-national company with known assets of fifty-squillion quid that decided to hang on to what was rightfully yours for as long as they could get away with it in order to squeeze out the last few pennies of interest.

Domestically the loss of my job was a considerable body blow; it added an element of uncertainty to our financial situation and put strain on a marriage that was already under pressure. There was, however, a glimmer of hope in that I had been given the opportunity to take all the current work load with me. What I had to do now was convince my clients that I could deliver as a freelance without the weight of a company behind me.

At the time I was working on commissions from ICI, Safeway, regional housing associations and several local companies, all of which were supportive. They would sustain my cash flow for the immediate future – but it was something entirely different that would dominate things and require a massive personal commitment.

A few years earlier in 1992, Middlesbrough had won recognition for the policies it was devising to make the town a more environmentally conscious place and encouraging partnership between the public, private and voluntary sectors to do this. These policies covered a range of activities from recycling to health, and included the landscape environment. As a result, together with the other winners Leeds, Leicester and Peterborough, Middlesbrough was awarded the title of 'Environment City' and the charitable status that went with it. During the previous few years, I had attended meetings of their environmental group in an unpaid, advisory capacity as it seemed to be good PR.

I rarely made much of a contribution but at one particular meeting I was very much centre stage. It was a warm sunny day and we were ploughing our way laboriously through the agenda. On reaching 'any other business', we started tossing around ideas to raise the profile of Middlesbrough Environment City (MEC). With very little forethought, and rather tongue in cheek, I suggested we mount an exhibit at the Chelsea Flower Show. I expected my suggestion to be met with a dozen good reasons not to do so, but I was wrong. Rather than being dismissed out of hand, the idea prompted serious discussion. When the meeting eventually finished, I had agreed to contact the Royal Horticultural Society (RHS) and had a brief to come up with some ideas. I was amazed and more than a little shocked.

The concept was simple: to produce a garden that reflected how Middlesbrough was emerging from the scars left by a hundred years of heavy industry, and how the various local environmental agencies were working with the natural environment to achieve this goal.

Realising this concept proved rather more difficult.

The next few weeks saw some febrile attempts to create an acceptable proposal that combined these aspects and would hopefully meet the exacting standards of the RHS. We were working on a wing and a prayer with no sponsorship in place and no experience of such events. Now that I think back, it was all pretty crazy. Anyway, I drew up the final design in early June and sent it off to the RHS. All we could do now was wait and hope.

In August the letter from the RHS dropped through my letter box. I opened it knowing that a rejection would be a disappointment but being realistic; with my business hat on (one that I don't possess, of course), it would probably be a blessing. As it turned out, it was neither a 'dear John' nor a letter of congratulations and I had to read it twice before fully understanding all its implications. Quite clearly we would not be building a set-piece show garden, but there was an invitation to submit a modified scheme along the lines of a themed exhibit within the grand marquee. Long story short, that is what we did and we were immediately accepted. Then the fun started.

Whilst we had the design element sorted out, we still hadn't secured sponsorship. As the year ebbed away, I became more and more anxious. To secure space at the Chelsea Flower Show is in itself an achievement so I suspected that failing to turn up would be an offence that could prompt the return of capital punishment. With the strong possibility of a death sentence hanging over us, my colleague at MEC and I worked hard in pursuing all the usual suspects in the north east.

Back in 1995 there were still several bastions of industry in our area, such as ICI and British Steel, but we soon found out that these companies were continually being pestered for sponsorship and were not easily persuaded. Reflecting on these names now, both of which have ceased to exist on Teesside, they were clearly not in a position to dish out funding, no matter how modest.

Those of you who have watched the Chelsea Flower Show on television will have heard exhibitors talk about how much planning and lead time their garden or display has taken to formulate. You have to think well in advance to arrange plant material of the quality required for the show. Our design incorporated a substantial number of wild flowers, all of which had to be grown from seed, and sections of yew hedge grown in containers and cut to specific shapes. We were having to commit all of the scarce funding offered by Middlesbrough Council to secure these key elements of the exhibit in the hope that a main sponsor would eventually come forward. We were flying by the seat of our pants and it was getting awfully chilly!

In the new year, and by now somewhat desperate, we decided to spread the net a little wider and talked to Northumbrian Water. At the time they were implementing substantial works to the River Tees to improve water quality, so their ethos was pertinent to our theme. Come February, a deal was struck. To my great relief, I was now in a position to start assembling the parts that would, hopefully, all come together in May.

As well as the wildflowers and trimmed yew hedges, the exhibit included four birch trees, sections of bespoke joinery, two pallets of clay pavers, a water feature and copious amounts of compost, all of which needed to be pre-ordered with exact delivery times. Then there were our special ingredients that we hoped would set our exhibit apart from all others: blast furnace slag, rusting industrial debris and orchids!

Just north of the Tees' estuary is a complex of heavy industrial sites. Over the latter half of the twentieth century these had laid waste vast tracts of land with all manner of detritus, including blast furnace slag, pulverised fly ash, lime gypsum and other nasties. These are not the locations you would normally expect to support any flora or fauna but, if you envelop them with a security fence as had been the case for many decades, all manner of wonderful things become possible.

The wildlife conservation group at MEC had been working with these industries for some time, notably ICI, and closely monitoring how some plants were now beginning to colonise sections of this waste land, most notably common marsh and spotted orchids.

Several weeks before the show, and with the blessing of ICI, a group of us spent half a day carefully lifting a small number of orchids and bagging up quantities of slag and items of rusting industrial junk. In a sense it was the very essence of our theme, illustrating how the landscape can recover given time and the stewardship of a more caring society.

With all the component parts sourced and a show pamphlet being printed, I turned my attention to logistics. How was I going to bring all this together, and how long would the process take?

The salient word in 'Chelsea Flower Show' is 'show'. Good horticultural practice is desirable, but when it comes to figuring out how you're going to build your design you are advised to think theatrical as much as horticultural. Unlike the show gardens outside, exhibits within the main marquee have to be built without excavations, so if you want to go down then first you have to go up. Quite often, hidden beneath the veneer of horticultural excellence, there is a lash-up of all manner of things strategically placed to raise levels and achieve that all-important third dimension.

The other great challenge is logistics, making sure that all the elements of your exhibit arrive at the right time to slot into the build. Organising this isn't too difficult – it's just that another two hundred exhibitors are doing the same thing. No matter how well you plan, it becomes pretty chaotic, rather like building a garden in the central reserve of the M6. During the build-up period there is a one-way traffic system around the site to facilitate deliveries but even then, with so many vehicles coming and going and hundreds of people focused on completing their own versions of perfection, it is impossible not to get a little fraught.

I'd calculated that our small team could construct the exhibit within three days. With the preview day set for Monday the 20th of May, the day of the royal visit together with VIPs and the press, I thought I should drive down on the Thursday of the previous week so I had time to prepare before the gang arrived on Friday.

Before I left, I gave my final briefing to our contractor, loaded my car with pretty much everything I felt we might need and set out on the long drive south. It was a hellish journey as I constantly considered the various scenarios and 'what ifs' of having overlooked some vital component or, worse still, some piece of security documentation.

When I arrived, I snaked my way around the one-way system. Everywhere I looked, display gardens were already taking shape. These were far more ambitious and complicated to construct than our more modest exhibit – or that's what I kept telling myself to allay my sudden feeling of panic.

I located our plot and then it hit me: I was a contributor, no matter how modest, to the most prestigious horticultural show in the country, perhaps even the world. The responsibility weighed very heavily.

I took a minute then unloaded the car and started pegging out the main features of our exhibit. That done, I joined the hustle of London's chaotic roads in search of my digs. The next day would be the start of a process that would test the planning and hard work of the last twelve months, so I turned in early feeling more than a little apprehensive and somewhat overwhelmed.

My alarm call next morning was the deafening roar of a jumbo jet a few hundred feet above the rooftops as it made its final descent into Heathrow Airport. I set off early to the showground and completed my preliminary setting out. As I drank a quick coffee in the exhibitors' café, I was joined by one of our suppliers. I sat chatting with Diarmuid Gavin and David Stevens; I knew David because we had both briefly attended a course at Thames Polytechnic. He later dropped out and became an eminent garden designer and author of several gardening books, whereas I went on to become a fully qualified and completely anonymous landscape architect! I hadn't a clue who Diarmuid Gavin was, though people kept telling me he was going to be a big name in garden design.

The team who were going to build the MEC exhibit turned up around midday and that is when, for me, things began to go pear shaped. For obvious reasons, I had suggested we use a local contractor. It was a relatively new business so the omens seemed right – a new company trying to make good impression etc. However, I was rather perturbed when the contractor and his team arrived with only half the required load of blocks, having not previously mentioned the carrying capacity of their vehicle. The blocks had been donated by Marshalls, who were based in Wakefield, so the only way we could get the rest was for someone to make a return trip up the M1.

This gave me a significant problem. I couldn't afford to take a man off the build, so there was only one thing for it – I have to make the journey myself. At the crack of dawn the next morning, I took the wagon and began the 350-mile round trip to Yorkshire. On reflection this was another mistake that became immediately apparent on my return.

A key element of the design was the way in which the paving blocks fitted within a series of timber retaining panels, so I was shocked to find someone with a Stihl saw cutting blocks, an activity that was causing some discomfort to our neighbouring exhibitors. Had I stayed, I could have told them to space them in order to take out any anomaly; after all, no one would actually be walking on them.

Come Saturday, we had the general structure in place and I started installing the fountain water feature. To my relief, it slotted in perfectly and we quickly filled, wired up and tested it. During the afternoon a wagon train of steel trolleys arrived containing our plants, thousands of them. From the moment they started arriving, I saw we had another problem: many of them were not fully in flower. This was another disappointment, but one about which I was a little more philosophical.

By selecting wild flowers, I had felt we were killing two birds with one stone: firstly they fulfilled our design criteria (the reparation of a damaged landscape), and secondly they would naturally be in flower at the right time for the Chelsea Flower Show. Mother Nature is notoriously fickle, however; in spring 1996 she decided to bless us with extremely cold and wet weather, which delayed the season by a couple of weeks.

My suppliers had attempted to bring them on but with only modest success. Some people can hold back bulbs so they flower for Chelsea and others can bring forward flowering plants such as roses, but it requires a lot of money to create artificial conditions to cheat the weather and it can only be done if you have the time to oversee every aspect of the operation. Sadly, this wasn't an option for us. I guess we were just unlucky in picking the wrong year.

Putting all the mishaps of the previous days behind me, I travelled to the showground on Sunday morning feeling more positive. The workmen had gone back to Yorkshire. The planting element of the exhibit required a more delicate touch and for that I called on the services of my wife.

We worked tirelessly during the day, distracted only momentarily when a freak gust of wind slammed through the marquee and split the top ridge beam directly above our heads with a terrifying crack. The hustle and bustle around us suddenly stopped and all eyes looked up, expecting to see timbers and canvas collapsing in on us. Fortunately that didn't happen but some essential repair work was required that impacted on our progress.

Even without this interruption, I could see we were falling behind the clock. We resumed the race against time. It was well after midnight when the last plant was placed carefully into the soft compost. There was a brief moment of great relief – but it was only brief because I knew that my car, parked in the exhibitors' car park across the river in Battersea Park, was now locked behind a pair of substantial gates. As we left the showground, I hadn't a clue how we were going to get back to Richmond.

My wife and I stood in the cool night air, casting an eye along an almost completely deserted Chelsea Embankment. Then a black cab appeared from out of nowhere and pulled up at the kerb as if it had been summoned. A pumpkin coach pulled by a team of white mice would have seemed equally plausible.

I collapsed into its warm interior knowing that the job was done. It had been hard and would not have happened without my wife's help. For all that subsequently went wrong between us (and for which I bear much responsibility), we always worked well together. Whether it was in our own garden or on an exhibit at the Chelsea Flower Show, we had an understanding the roots of which were grounded in our love

147

for what we were doing and a desire to do it well.

Early next morning, my wife returned to Yorkshire while I donned suit and tie for preview day and the evening gala. In 1996 this charity event, attended by the great and the good, included me and a bloke from Northumbrian Water.

Inexplicably the Queen's entourage didn't visit our exhibit but the day still had its moments. There was some excitement at a neighbouring stand where the lovely Jane Asher appeared, surrounded by cameras, to promote a rose named in her honour.

Later, there was a very special moment for me. I became aware of a couple taking a particular interest in the four birch trees we had used; the man seemed vaguely familiar. Well, I'll be... It was George Harrison!

I wandered over to see if I could help. My thoughts were along the lines of 'Can I lick your shoes clean for you?', but I found myself talking horticultural matters. For you gardening buffs, we were discussing the fact that the bark of silver birch trees is often bronze coloured until they become more mature.

I've reflected on that moment many times. The thing that is most precious to me is that we had something we were both interested in where we were equals – and I am so proud of the fact I didn't trouble him for an autograph! Many years later, I discovered that my old mucker George, as I now called him, was a keen gardener. I'd like to think he was genuinely interested in my nervous explanation.

Around five o'clock, the VIPs and press were ushered out to be replaced by the society brigade, most of whom are not interested in horticulture but *must* be seen at the gala, the first stop on London's annual merry-go-round of society bunfights. I can't be too scathing as it is an event that benefits a diverse number of charities, but at that moment a show that once was a mecca for the enthusiast, was being usurped by hype and nonsense. In the intervening thirty years I have seen nothing to change my mind.

As the gala ended, I started thinking about the day ahead which was of far greater importance to me: the opening of the show to the public and the day I'd find out how the RHS had assessed our modest exhibit.

⊙ ⊙ ⊙

The following morning, I entered the marquee and saw medal certificates perched on the various stands. When I arrived at ours, I hardly dare look. It had been given an award but I was terribly disappointed that it was only a bronze medal. Suddenly the anxieties of the last ten months and the exhaustion of the final week sapped away my spirits and I just wanted to go home.

My desolation lifted a little when Carol Klein (not then a household name but already a multi-medal winner) approached me and asked how we'd got on. She could see my disappointment and she was kind enough to offer a few words of consolation, pointing out that a bronze medal as a Chelsea debutante was nothing to be ashamed of.

Her comments helped put things into perspective. I decided to take up the offer of speaking with the judges, something all exhibitors are entitled to do. As I'd suspected, we were marked down heavily for some of our plants not being in full flower. I can understand that – after all, it is a flower show – but I'm not sure they fully understood what we were about, something that dawned on me as I looked at other councils' exhibits.

The exhibits from Southend and Birmingham were brilliantly presented; Southend's featured a beach hut and Birmingham's was a car made out of tiny plants. They were not to my taste but they were brilliantly staged representations of these places. Like all the others, our submission was vetted before the show, but I can't help feeling the judges were a little surprised to see blast furnace slag and various items of industrial *objet d'rust* that were central to the story we were trying to tell.

My suspicions that small 'c' conservatism was in action were further aroused when I stumbled upon Diarmuid Gavin's garden, which he'd said was inspired by the interior of a public toilet in Dublin. It seemed that glass bricks and stainless steel, like slag and rusty stuff, had no place at Chelsea in 1996. He was awarded nothing. I thought, 'This guy is going nowhere,' but of course he did; glass bricks, stainless steel and the like have since become de rigueur at the show.

The week of the show was an anticlimax. Planning and building the exhibit had been totally absorbing and exciting as we made decisions and met deadlines to create something that had previously existed only in my mind's eye. With that adrenalin rush behind me, time seemed to drag and the week ahead loomed like a life sentence. But our modest little exhibit caught the eye of the press; Graham Rice, writing in the *Evening Standard*, gave us a mention when he listed his personal highlights, and the official show DVD also made reference to us.

For those of you who have not experienced the Chelsea Show, I should make some effort to describe the scene. The grounds of the Royal Hospital, Chelsea, (home to the Chelsea Pensioners) are not vast, so when you fill them with show gardens, commercial trade stands, glasshouses, marquees, refreshment tents and every conceivable bit of horticultural 'gotwhatary' you can think of, it tends to get a bit claustrophobic. During peak periods there is a tsunami feel about the place as people pour around the exhibits in the main marquee via a one-way system. If anyone wants to strike up a conversation with you, they need to jostle their way out of the throng.

A man from Middlesbrough detached himself from the crowd to regale me with his life history, which was all very interesting except that he positioned himself in such a way as to prevent me from talking to Angela Rippon, who was standing a few feet away studying my handiwork. If he'd moved a few inches, I could have impressed her with how I'd single-handedly turned Middlesbrough from a grey industrial wasteland into the Garden of Eden, and then charm her with a poem I'd written for the front of our pamphlet. It read:

Meanwhile, at social industry's command
How quick, how vast an increase! From the germ
Of some poor hamlet, rapidly produced
Here a huge town, continuous and compact,

Hiding the face of earth for leagues – and there,
Where not a habitation stood before,
Abodes of men irregularly massed
Like trees in forests, - spread through spacious tracts
O'er which the smoke of unremitting fires
Hangs permanent, and plentiful as wreaths
Of vapour glittering in the morning sun,
And, wheresoe'er the traveller turns his steps,
He sees the barren wilderness erased,
Or disappearing...

Okay, so it's Wordsworth, but Angela might not have known that.

The final day arrived and I looked forward to being joined by my family, whose arrival was closely followed by a deluge of rain. By the time the bell sounded for the end of the show, I was totally exhausted.

At this point a frantic tussle breaks out between desperate punters in an unholy rush to purchase items they could probably buy more cheaply at their local garden centre. I've seen people heading to Sloane Square tube station carrying trees or jumping on buses with impossible loads of garden plants. I wasn't interested; I scooped up my family and headed off out across a wet and windy Battersea Bridge in search of my car, leaving the heart-breaking business of pulling everything apart to our small workforce.

Looking back some twenty years later, I am philosophical about the whole episode. I designed and built an exhibit at the UK's premier horticultural show with only a modest budget, so there was no point in beating myself up over the lack of a gold medal. Maybe there are many things I'd do differently now, but I remain protective of our aim. More importantly, I felt privileged to be part of this wonderful event, and share the warmth and camaraderie of those taking part. It was a remarkable experience.

25

DIANA

THE following summer the nation was stunned by one of those terrible events for which there is no rhyme or reason, and for which we can never be prepared: Princess Diana was killed in a car crash in Paris.

Sixteen years had passed since Charles and Diana celebrated their wedding in 1981. That was an occasion that lifted the spirits during a troubled economic and social time. As we watched the grand ceremony, there was a sense of hope; it was a day to celebrate. Sadly, it proved to be a less than perfect match that resulted in a rather undignified separation just over ten years later

Diana was the beautiful young princess looking to the future, while Charles represented a royal household that seemed increasingly out of step with modern Britain. Her positive influence was apparent but seemed to be too much too soon. On the 31st of August 1997, all of this would be consigned to history and legacy.

You will probably recall the massive outpouring of public grief symbolised by more than a million floral tributes left outside Kensington Palace and the thousands of people who lined the streets for her funeral. I am generally uncomfortable with mass public displays of emotion where dignity and solemnity are often overtaken by something of a grief fest. But not here; there was a genuine sense of loss. The 'people's princess', as Prime Minister Tony Blair referred to her, was gone.

The funeral service at Westminster Abbey included a musical eulogy from Diana's long-time friend, Elton John. His rendition of 'Goodbye England's Rose', a rework of 'Candle In The Wind' could have been painfully crass but instead it was poignant and clearly delivered with sincerity.

There is so much that could be written about Princess Diana, but I think it best if I leave her life in the hands of the biographers. Her charisma tended to eclipse what some saw as a rather staid monarchy. Her short life was very much to be celebrated, not least for all the charitable work she undertook in support of causes that were difficult, challenging and in some cases downright dangerous.

Diana was a child of the aristocracy but always appeared approachable. She used her position of privilege positively and invariably made a good impression with the public, something the senior royals found more difficult, weighed down as they were by outdated protocol.

It is difficult to know how Diana's death impacted on them beyond their natural feelings of grief, but it did appear to redefine their relationship with the public. Sadly, it was only after her premature demise that her influence has become truly apparent as her sons seem set to redefine the institution that is our royalty.

26

A LABOUR OF LOVE

MY post-Chelsea anticlimax was aided and abetted by my old Achilles' heel: my inability to promote my skills. Garden design tends to be at the 'showbiz' end of what I do, and those who specialise in the art tend to be extrovert and comfortable in blowing their own trumpets. I am not of that breed. Most of my work has been associated with landscape amenity projects, an area of expertise for which I am better equipped. The problem is that, whether you design gardens or city parks as a freelance consultant, you still need to promote your abilities. My ongoing failure to do this has put something of a brake on my professional career.

After Chelsea, my attention quickly returned to landscape projects. I gained commissions from the Royal Mail, ICI and Bellway Homes, all good names for the CV, but the work was rarely challenging. Most of the projects I've undertaken in my freelance career have been bread and butter stuff, though that is of little concern to me. I've regarded all work, no matter how modest or seemingly insignificant, as a personal design challenge for which I must produce a solution I believe in.

My old tutor back in Leeds constantly haunts me with his catchy mission statement, '*Sort it out, for Christ's sake. There's people out there in the rain.*' It is an adage that anyone involved with design should remember; whether they are designing landscape, cars or furniture, it is a cross any self-respecting designer should be prepared to bear. It is one that has given me many a sleepless night, but it has always been worth it

I've referred to the broad scope of work undertaken by professional landscape architects. I have never questioned the motivational force behind this – but *why* do I feel such immense job satisfaction? Why does the natural landscape excite me, and what hold does it have over me that I feel the need and passion to care for it? What exactly makes it such a labour of love?

There is a wealth of literature to substantiate my love of plants, gardens and the wider landscape, and the physical and psychological relationship we have with them. Such matters have exercised the minds and caused the creative juices to flow in poets and authors from Shakespeare to Oscar Wilde and D. H. Lawrence. Even the Bible has its moments: *Songs of Solomon*, chapter 5, verses 12–16, (New International Version) describes a courtship in very florid text.

He says:

(12) You are a garden locked up, my sister, my bride; you are a spring enclosed, a sealed fountain.

(13) Your plants are an orchard of pomegranates with choice fruits, with henna and nard,

(14) nard and saffron, calamus and cinnamon, with every kind of incense tree, with myrrh and aloes and all the finest spices.

(15) You are a garden fountain, a well of flowing water streaming down from Lebanon.

Even without knowing what nard is, you'd have to admit it's an exceptionally cool chat-up line.

She replies:

(16) Awake, north wind, and come south wind! Blow on my garden, that its fragrance may spread everywhere. Let my beloved come into his garden and taste its choice fruits.

I'll leave you to investigate the literary side of things while I examine this relationship through the visual arts. Nothing matches the experience of the real thing but a well-executed image, albeit two dimensional, has the potential to draw the observer into a given location and immerse them within it, giving them the concept and psychology of spatial, contextual awareness.

I am drawn to the French Baroque artists, whose romantic depictions of figures cloistered within landscapes strewn with classical temples, castles and ruins informed the designs of William Kent, Capability Brown and Humphry Repton a century later. They were the pioneers of what would eventually become known as the English style of garden design.

Historically, Studley Royal near Ripon pre-dates the works of Capability Brown and company but it was almost certainly a precursor to their particular brand of English landscape/garden design. Set within a section of the Skell river valley, its densely wooded and craggy flanks provide a beautiful, natural enclosure that is both dramatic and secluded. It is a place where I can commune with my surroundings by way of some primal interaction, enclosed in what feels like a verdant womb. Add to that John Aislaby's romantic water garden, embellished with architectural follies and sculptural features, and you will find yourself in a landscape that gives a tangible sense of place with a magnitude that would have Claude Lorrain's brushes twitching with excitement.

Aislaby's son, William, later extended the garden to include an existing ruin, a must for all the best gardens of this period. This was no ordinary ruin, it was Fountains Abbey, a Cistercian stronghold for more than four hundred years until Henry VIII's wrecking ball converted it into arguably the most romantic demolition site in the UK. Take a walk along the south/west ridge and stumble upon the so-called 'surprise view' of the abbey. I imagine the secluded seat, positioned in order to take full advantage of this beautiful view, has borne witness to many a proposal of marriage.

In recent times, and especially since its designation as a world heritage site, Fountains Abbey and its water gardens have become victims of their own success. To fully appreciate their beauty, I suggest avoiding peak opening hours. Sharing the experience with hundreds of families, coach loads of humanity and an assortment of dogs rather compromises the experience. Make the effort to go off peak and out of season and I challenge you not to feel moved by it. It is a very special experience.

⊙⊙⊙

Man's manipulation of the landscape is only half the story; there is also the magic of Mother Nature herself and her powerful ability to renew. This played a spectacular role in another project I encountered a few years later. It came in the form of a nine-hole golf academy to be set on the Tees' flood plain at Ingleby Barwick, defined by a huge meander in the river's course. Its former use as agricultural land had been abandoned because of expanding residential development and the social knock-on effects.

Along its southern margin the river valley rises abruptly into an escarpment where an old quarry, now densely wooded, had been designated as a nature reserve. I worked with a specialist designer to create a course that was both challenging to the golfer and also sympathetic to the existing landscape and wildlife habitat. We wanted to enhance both by creating a series of water bodies linked into the River Tees.

A battalion of bulldozers, scrapers and trucks trundled onto the land and started to do their worst – and they did. I was astonished at how far my colleague was prepared to go in his quest to squeeze every last drop of golfing experience from the landscape. He spent the best part of six months on site waving his arms about like a man possessed, directing digger drivers to create new ponds and orchestrating the movements of mighty machines to reshape the landscape into greens, fairways and tees. By autumn, the once-benign pastoral scene had been transformed into something resembling a battlefield. It was then left to overwinter, allowing me time to supervise the tree planting before spring when more machinery arrived to till the ground for grass seeding.

Then the magic happened. I remember standing at the highest point on the course with the managing director of the company whose team had, for the last half year, knocked the crap out of the place. The panorama that just a few months previously looked so dismal was now transformed by sweeping mounds, swales and glistening waters. It was adorned with a mantle of green and you couldn't fail to sense the new life all around it.

This is the time of year when nature's healing ability is at its most powerful, and it is at the very essence of all that I've done in pursuing my profession. I feel privileged in having a career that has allowed me to appreciate the immense power of this phenomenon year after year.

Tatanka Yotanke (Sitting Bull), head of the Lakota Sioux, put this feeling rather more poetically, stating:

'*Behold my brothers, the spring has come; the earth has received the embraces of the sun and we shall soon see the results of that love! Every seed is awakened and so has all animal life. It is through this mysterious power that we too have our being and we therefore yield to our neighbours, even our animal neighbours, the same right as ourselves, to inhabit this land.*'

Striking a rapport with one's surroundings is a special thing: it heightens the senses to the gifts of nature and an appreciation of the natural environment and all that it contains.

I make no defence for my eccentricities and I am grateful I've been so afflicted. I've tried to describe my feelings over the last few pages but if my rather awkward, self-absorbed, approach doesn't strike a note with you, how about this for a bit of carousing with nature? Kim Wilde, eighties' pop singer and latter-day garden designer commented: '*I don't take myself seriously any more, sometimes I just garden in my knickers and platform shoes!*'

It's a long way from Shakespeare, Oscar Wilde and D. H. Lawrence, but I'm sure she is probably experiencing that same intrinsic oneness with the environment.

27

TECHNOLOGICAL REVOLUTION #2
MILLENNIUM BUG

IT was the summer of 1999 and I was standing with my daughter at the Trocadero, looking across the Seine to the Eiffel Tower where a huge digital clock was relentlessly counting down time to the Millennium. It brought home very graphically something that had been haunting me for a number of years: my fiftieth birthday.

If it wasn't difficult enough watching my daughter racing headlong into adolescence, I also had to face up to becoming a fully paid-up member of the old gits' club. Previous birthdays with a big zero hadn't really bothered me: thirty was no sweat and I was in my prime; life begins at forty... But fifty? That was seriously old and a prospect I found extremely alarming.

My only comfort was that many of my contemporaries appeared to be in denial and had avoided cavalry-twill trousers, woollen cardigans and all things beige that seemed to epitomise the middle-aged man of previous generations. We had Eric Clapton, Status Quo, The Rolling Stones and, most importantly, denim. Maybe, just maybe, I would not be afflicted by the curse of sartorial atrophy. I lived in hope.

Unfortunately the same couldn't be said for my private life and professional prospects. As the old century ebbed away, so did my optimism. My life was running away from me in directions it should not have been going, and I was heading toward my personal take on a mid-life crisis. But someone somewhere must have been looking out for me because, totally out of the blue, I received a call from a former work colleague. He had returned to his native Hartlepool, where he had established a practice called Landmark Partnership. His existing partner wanted out and I was invited to take his place. I began yet another phase in my career.

⊙⊙⊙

As we neared the end of the decade, millennium fever broke out like a rash. Where were you going to be and what would you be doing? People were besotted with one single moment in time, and some had been making arrangements months (even years) in advance. I would not be on top of the Eiffel Tower, crossing the equator or partying at the Savoy; instead, I looked forward to joining family and friends at the village celebrations.

As the evening came to an end, we walked home and I attempted to light the bonfire I'd prepared but that had been rendered pretty much fireproof by a period of steady rain. We retired to the house and switched on the television to watch highlights of the fireworks' display along the Thames. They turned out to be equally pathetic; the 'River of Fire' proved to be about as exciting as a boy-scout campfire on a canoe, though slightly less entertaining. Fortunately the display at Sydney Harbour was sensational, so thank you Australia for saving the millennium!

The first days and weeks of the twenty-first century passed into history and the dreaded fiftieth birthday arrived. A surprise birthday party had been arranged, calling in lots of old friends and acquaintances to share my celebration, but below the surface I was feeling a deep sadness.

I suddenly became conscious of the passing years. My parents had aged and my father was starting to lose his battle with Parkinson's disease that he'd been fighting for many years. My mother was bravely coping with the stress of his failing health. My friends, some of whom I hadn't seen for more than twenty years, were no longer the fresh-faced mates I remembered. When the party was over and everyone had left, I took a moment to look at the book that had been compiled for me. It depicted a life with highs and lows like thousands of others and prompted recollections of happy moments and those tinged with regret.

⊙⊙⊙

Despite predictions of computer bugs and all manner of apocalyptic events, the new millennium began without incident. For the Landmark Partnership, things were on the up as we had secured a massive commission from Hartlepool Council. This involved preparing a qualitative landscape assessment for the whole council district to assist in matters of development control and general planning issues. The only problem was that we didn't have the manpower, the IT or the IT skills to deliver such a huge and complicated undertaking. Secure in the knowledge of the income the work would generate, we went shopping for computers and some temporary staff who knew their Asus from their Epson.

I've always been wary of computer technology. I'd managed to dodge the issue over the last ten years, but I could sense it behind me like a tidal wave. Come the new millennium, it had become an unstoppable force and I resigned myself to the inevitable.

The impact on our everyday working and domestic lives was unprecedented. Though I have largely resisted, I can now Google with the best of them and I concede it is something I could not have done without whilst compiling my scrapbook.

However, I'm not a slave to it and never will be. I accept that computers are essential if we are to sustain our itinerant and rapidly growing population and the huge volume of transactions that this generates. The advent of computer-aided design (CAD) has revolutionised our manufacturing and construction industries. My reservations about computer technology are prompted by two considerations. First is the vulnerability of many of these systems to criminals who consider the term 'failsafe' as a personal challenge. Second, and this particularly applies to design software, is that the tail can start to wag the dog. I have seen how CAD can help the design process, but the clue to its functionality is in the name: computer *aided* design. It is a tool, albeit a sophisticated one, not something that can supplant the intellectual processes and flair of the designer. I wonder if sometimes the convenience of CAD is detrimental to creativity and therefore to design quality.

For me, conveying my design ideas through my ability to draw is very precious. It is the one gift I've been given and I am very protective of it. Hand-drawn plans say a great deal about their creators and I have always taken great pride in producing them, whether they are master plans, design details or conceptual perspective sketches. Now those skills are being sidelined by computers and, as a result, architects' plans tend to look the same no matter who produces them.

We must be very careful not to diminish our potential by allowing computerisation to override our thought processes. Yes, we need computers and working guidelines in our hectic world, but we cannot become slaves to them. We must be able to deal with the complexities of life with their assistance, not their domination. Of course, coming from a self-confessed technophobe such as myself, I realise it is very easy for the computer-iety to dismiss my claims, so I'll defer to one better placed to do so: Stephen Hawking.

There is a real danger that computers will develop intelligence and take over. We urgently need to develop direct connections to the brain so that computers can add to human intelligence rather than be in opposition.

I appreciate the benefits of computer aided design; in the hands of a professional designer, it can be an extraordinarily useful tool. But I worry that this and a million and one other apps may falsely empower laypeople into believing they can dispense with the services of trained professionals.

⊙⊙⊙

The much-anticipated millennium had come and gone. It was something I had dreaded because it seemed to be the portent of old age, but it was a mere moment. I soldiered on in a changing world I barely recognised, a fact brought home to me every time I looked at the book that had been prepared for my birthday.

My comfortable analogue existence of books, vinyl records, telephones, drawing boards and etiquette was being swept aside by a brash impersonal world dependant on computer technology, and at the expense of culture, dexterous skills and the concept of thinking for one's self. It transpired that the real bug – my fear of being fifty – was less to do with the possible onset of conservative knitwear and polyester blazers and rather more to do with being left behind in time.

28

9/11 - TRYING TO COMPREHEND
THE INCOMPREHENSIBLE

THE 9th of September 2001 seemed like an ordinary day at the office. I was working at my drawing board when news broke about the attack on the World Trade Centre in New York. It wasn't until I returned home that I saw the true horror and the appalling carnage.

The whole attack was incomprehensible to any sane being. After the trauma, anger and grief came the inevitable question: why had innocent citizens, going about their business in New York, been targeted in such a despicable way?

Many believed it was a response from Islamic fundamentalist groups, spearheaded by al Qaeda, to American foreign policy that was seen as beneficial to the USA (and the West in general) at the expense of the Arab/Muslim nations. I can find little fault with that logic, chilling as it may be. We also have to factor in many years of western foreign policy, starting with the Crusades of the eleventh, twelfth and thirteenth centuries through to Victorian imperialism, the indiscriminate partitioning of the former Ottoman Empire and imposition of the state of Israel in 1948. It has been a turbulent and confrontational history, fired by religious intolerance that has often resulted in ungodly campaigns of hatred, bigotry and violence. This is not the place for levity, yet I am drawn to the comedy genius Billy

Connolly who commented: '*A lot of people are too easily offended. Religious people for instance. They've been offending other people for centuries.*'

I think he has it about right.

In the UK, we have become fairly apathetic toward any form of religious fervour. Yes, Billy Graham's occasional visits stirred up a little evangelical zeal, prompting the appearance of a few holy rollers and happy-clappy tambourine bashers, but it never amounted to much. A sad exception to this apathy was the unrest in Northern Ireland, but the sectarian differences supposedly at the heart of that confrontation are now more often re-enacted via sporting events, which in Scotland means the 'old firm' football match between Rangers (Protestant) versus Celtic (Catholic). How many of the fans claiming partisanship based on religious difference can be found practising their beliefs in church the next morning? Judging by church attendance figures for either denomination in the UK, very few.

I think it is a shame that the church *per se* has fallen out of step with contemporary life and its ceremonies have become remote from our busy lives. I am convinced there is a need for places of salvation and contemplation, as I discovered many years ago when I spent a little time in Florence. I decided to visit the Basilica Santa Croce because it contains the tombs of Galileo, Michelangelo and Rossini rather than any quest for enlightenment. I was struck by the number of people on their way home from work who wanted nothing more than a few moments of peace, to light a candle and sit quietly with their thoughts. It was wonderful to see a place of religion being used personally and with dignity, rather than with great communal pomp and ceremony.

Unfortunately, our ambivalence toward religious belief does little to ingratiate us with more radical people elsewhere. We also start to run into difficulties when reflecting on economies and lifestyle, notably those enjoyed by the USA and Western Europe as opposed to the Islamic states of the Middle East and North Africa. Through the eyes of these people, I suspect capitalist western society appears profligate, materialistic and decadent. I would find it difficult to make a cogent argument to counter such resentment.

However, resentment is one thing. When this degenerates into the clutches of extremists who are prepared to enslave women, rape and carry out mass murder and public executions as part of their doctrine, there is a serious problem.

⊙⊙⊙

During my lifetime, the relationship between East and West has been played out through conflict and violence. In 1967, though essentially a regional dispute, and not involving western forces, the Six-Day War between Israel and Egypt was symptomatic of the problem that had been exacerbated by our intervention and gerrymandering which initially created the nation state of Israel. Seventeen years later, WPC Yvonne Fletcher was murdered by a single shot from the Libyan Embassy in London. Three years after that, on the 21st of December 1988, centuries of animosity were again visited upon our shores when Pan Am Flight 103 was bombed out of the sky above the small Scottish border town of Lockerbie, killing 243 passengers, sixteen aircrew and eleven people on the ground. Here again it was a cowardly and callous act perpetrated upon innocent people; in this instance, we believe the instigator was the Libyan leader, Colonel Gaddafi, whose difficult relationship with the UK and the western world was obvious. But what set of circumstances can trigger such hatred and the wilful murder of innocent subjects?

Sadly, in the case of the 9/11 attack, the Bush–Blair alliance gave the pot another stir by deploying troops to Afghanistan in an attempt to destroy the governing Taliban, who, it was felt, were harbouring Osama bin Laden and the al Qaeda radicals deemed responsible for the attacks on the World Trade Centre. In doing so, they clearly did not consider the Soviet Union's attempts to do the same throughout the eighties, which ended in failure and the loss of over a million Afghan lives. On that occasion the USA was actually backing the Mujahideen in Afghanistan, the forerunners of the Taliban, rather than fighting them, the Mujahideen being deemed less hateful than the 'old enemy',

Soviet Russia. Gets confusing, doesn't it?

Having failed to flush out bin Laden, Bush and Blair turned their attentions once again to Iraq, accusing Saddam Hussein's regime of cooperating with al Qaeda and possessing weapons of mass destruction (WMD). Neither claim was substantiated, despite their probing; in fact, all evidence pointed to the contrary. The speech by US Secretary of State Donald Rumsfeld on the 12th of February 2002 was clearly worded to throw would-be doubters off the scent:

'Reports that say that something hasn't happened are always interesting to me, because as we know, there are known knowns; there are things we know we know. We also know there are known unknowns; that is to say we know there are some things we do not know. But there are also unknown unknowns – the ones we don't know we don't know. And if one looks throughout the history of our country and other free countries, it is the latter category that tend to be difficult ones'.

No WMDs were actually discovered, but that was discounted by Bush and Blair who sanctioned the military invasion of Iraq, supposedly in order to remove the tyrannical leadership of Saddam Hussein (which it did), and to bring peace and stability to the Iraqi nation (which it manifestly didn't). In the vacuum left behind following the invasion, radical Islamists elements within Iraq joined with like-minded fundamentalist factions within Syria to form an even greater threat: the so-called Islamic State of Iraq and Syria (ISIS), whose evil and barbaric doings have been beyond all reason.

Both America and Britain retained peace-keeping forces in Iraq. British forces were eventually withdrawn after six years, by which time 179 service personnel had lost their lives. Richard Thompson's song of 2007, 'Dad's Gonna Kill Me', written from the perspective of a soldier, reflects on the lot of a serviceman in Iraq, 'Dad' in the song being Baghdad. It describes a series of troubling and disturbing scenarios and highlights the terrors faced by the troops.

In pursuing these ill-conceived, some might say reckless, campaigns the Bush–Blair alliance did little to resolve the situation; in fact, they were probably instrumental in provoking various retaliatory actions

167

around the world, including the attacks on London in 2005 – often referred to as 7/7 – in which fifty-two civilians lost their lives.

By way of reflecting on this sombre and perplexing period, I suggest you seek out a couple of films, notably *Fahrenheit 9/11* and *Shock and Awe*. Both reveal the hypocrisy of the Bush administration, *Fahrenheit 9/11* particularly so in its damning of the Bush family. It exposes them for having business links with the bin Ladens and dealings with the off-shore bank known as the Bank of Credit and Commerce International (BCCI). As far as Prime Minister Tony Blair is concerned, I hope there are no similar skeletons in the cupboard. His crime, as I see it, was one of collusion through gutless compliance and cosying up to the American leadership.

In the wake of these events, the USA elected a new president, Barack Obama, and the UK a new Prime Minister, David Cameron. The fact that Obama was the first African American to hold the presidency gave many of us reason to be optimistic, not least because in his first period in office he visited Cairo to deliver a speech entitled 'A New Beginning'. The message was simple enough: he wanted to ease East–West tensions, and create a better understanding with the Islamic states. But he didn't shy away from telling it like it was, and amongst the warm, conciliatory speak came a few passages that would have been more difficult for some of his audience to swallow. To mention '*principles of justice and progress; tolerance and the dignity of all human beings*', and that people should have '*the ability to speak their mind and have a say in how they are governed*', were concepts of democracy that would have rankled with the dictators and religious zealots still holding sway in several Islamic states.

Not surprisingly, his speech got a mixed reception but in its wake, though not necessarily as a result of it, came the so-called 'Arab Spring'. People in several Islamic nations rebelled, only for most of them to be crushed by the aforementioned dictators, often with much bloodshed. Civil war erupted in Libya in 2011; such was the human carnage that the United Nations, with the agreement of the Arab League, gave its blessing for military intervention. The UK, France and Canada obliged with air strikes following a missile onslaught from British and US naval forces. Six months later, David Cameron and French President Sarkozy were welcomed like heroes in Benghazi, with Cameron stating, '*it's great to be in free Libya*'. However, despite the troublesome Gaddafi being deposed and we Brits being hailed as peacemakers, all the initiative seemed to achieve was to clear the way for further disagreements amongst Islamic factions that culminated in further unrest and another civil war.

A few months after the removal of Gadaffi, President Obama ordered a strategic raid within Pakistan that successfully took out Osama bin Laden, the person deemed responsible for the 9/11 attack on the New York Trade Centre. It was an action widely applauded around the world, including much of the Middle East, but violence and mayhem remain a fact of life from Tunisia in the west to Pakistan in the east, despite Obama's further attempts to improve relations.

Sadly, I think his achievements on the world stage have been largely overlooked or downplayed by a nation that still sees itself as *the* super power of the world. In this context, his draw-down of troops from Afghanistan and Iraq, and his efforts to reboot the USA as a more conciliatory member of the world community, have been judged by his Republican opponents as a sign of weakness. They have used them to make political propaganda to appeal to the more extremist, jingoistic elements within American society.

By contrast, other than a few loony, right-wing sabre rattlers, we modern Brits seem to have overcome the notion that we somehow 'rule the waves'. But what are the Brits and what is Great Britain? Technically, Great Britain is the landmass of England, Wales and Scotland, it being the larger (greater) of the British Isles. However, use of the word 'great' is often misinterpreted as some sort of nationalistic self-aggrandisement. Perhaps it is time to address this problem. Let our nation, including Northern Ireland, be known simply as Britain, thereby simultaneously dispensing with the rather ambiguous 'United Kingdom' and dispelling any international misconceptions.

As I see it, such action is part of maturing as an equal, one-body nation within the world community – a concept that seems beyond the comprehension of many Americans.

⊙ ⊙ ⊙

How can the parties to these tragedies extinguish the deep-seated resentment that spans centuries? I think it would help if all nations made a better effort to understand other cultures rather than perpetuate constant fear fostered by ignorance. Similarly, we need to start living our lives with compassion and not at the expense of others. At the very least we need to have respect for the history, traditions and religious beliefs of other nations and to abide by their laws when we visit them. Obviously this ideology needs to be reciprocated: respect and compassion are central to *all* true religions. This is no better exemplified than by the words of Mohammad who taught his followers: *'Be merciful to others and you will receive mercy. Forgive others and Allah will forgive you.'*

Sadly, the situation in the Middle East remains volatile. Huge numbers of people from Syria, Iraq and North African nations are fleeing for their lives to escape the brutality of dictators and fundamentalists whose resentment of the West we have done little to assuage. Our response to the situation – or at least the response of the European Union – has, to date, been undeniably weak and lamentably incoherent.

29

A FEW MINUTES OF FAME

IN 2002 the Landmark Partnership became just Landmark. The practice was losing out to larger companies because we lacked the capacity to deliver larger, more lucrative projects; at the same time, we could not survive on small jobs. We needed to adapt and did this by way of an amicable agreement that released my partner to take a new position elsewhere and me to take ownership of the name Landmark, plus the associated goodwill.

It was the beginning of yet another phase of my professional career. Before we had relinquished the keys to our office, things took another unexpected turn. By chance I heard that the BBC was looking for someone to project-manage a garden build in Leeds as part of the second series of its *Small Town Gardens Show*. In a moment of insanity, rather like Yozzer Hughes from *Boys from The Blackstuff*, I contacted them and said, '*I can do that, gizza job, go on, gizza job,*' or words to that effect. To my great surprise they did. A few weeks later I received the designer's plans and an instruction to visit the garden in question.

The client's favourite holiday destination was Morocco and they had requested a garden design that reflected the style of that country. A Moroccan style garden in north Leeds? The clients had already begun the unlikely transformation by building high garden walls finished with a cream render and clay copings. These gave a bit of a nod in the direction of Casablanca but looked at odds with the imposing

Victorian, stone-built house. The garden itself was a mish-mash; there were bits of this and bits of that where they had started and, by their own admission, been unsuccessful in creating a Moroccan Shangri-la. In addition, a large heap of topsoil occupied one corner, apparently left by the wall builders.

By now I was having some serious reservations about the whole project. The plans provided by the show's featured designers did little to allay my fears. They included a sizeable octagonal sunken area, plus a water feature as its central feature. I could see at a glance that its construction would take more manpower than the three university students assigned to me by the BBC.

To avoid committing to an undeliverable build, I decided to put down a few markers with the producer. Firstly, and most urgently, I needed more information from the designers to work out how to build the thing and to assess the quantities of materials we would need. Secondly, I needed a mini-digger and driver for a couple of days, together with a builder. Thirdly, I wanted to be sure that we would not encounter underground services when we excavated to the depth shown on the plans. I didn't want a member of my team sticking a pickaxe through an electricity cable and lighting up like a Roman candle.

My caution was not misplaced: electricity cables *did* run beneath the garden! This presented me with a major problem because the lead in to filming did not allow time for the electricity company to divert them and the budget wouldn't cover the additional cost involved.

I realised that the same sunken-garden effect could be achieved if we lifted the base level above the services. That would still provide the enclosure they wanted for the sunken area and had the bonus of creating informal seating around the outside as the top of the walls would be above ground level. I discussed it with the designers and managed to sell the idea – not that they had any option.

I went down to Leeds to meet the production team and the show's presenter, Joe Swift. This first visit was to film the 'reveal', where the designers would unveil their design to the client. It was a piece of filming that didn't include me but it gave me the opportunity to meet everyone with whom I'd be working.

In making these programmes there is a strict build period – in this case the 27th of May to the 14th of June – during which time the work is to be completed. Several filming dates are scheduled within this period, some of which the designers and presenter attend. The first is the reveal, then a couple of 'work in progress' shoots and finally the finished garden. On these days, building work takes second place to filming. There are also more informal shoots where the director and a small team film background material.

With all the introductions made and the reveal out of the way, it was time to roll up our sleeves and start the unglamorous business of breaking up concrete and filling skips.

Within a couple of days we had the garden stripped out so we could start implementing the new design, but the British weather had other ideas. It started raining – not just your ten-minute, springtime shower variety but full-on monsoon cloudbursts. The lost hours became lost days, precious time that we couldn't afford to lose. Eventually there was a bit of a break and the cavalry arrived in the form of our builder and the man with a mini-digger. In little over a day they completed the excavations and installed a drainpipe to the sunken area, an essential requirement but again something that had been conspicuously absent from the design plans. It would have taken days to do this manually.

Mercifully, the following day started fine and bright. We were going to cast the slab floor to the sunken area and I was counting on having a few hours' preparation time before the ready-mix man arrived. He turned up early and was not impressed by the prospect of having to wait a few minutes.

I'm sure some of you have watched shows such as *Challenge Anneka* and *DIY SOS* where good-hearted folk give time, donate materials or simply muck in to create playgrounds for kids or improvements to homes that would benefit their invalid occupants. Clearly our man with the ready-mix truck hadn't seen them; he shot the cement into an empty skip and scarpered, leaving us to barrow it in as quickly as we could.

During the next few days we managed to get some work done by dodging in and out of yet more torrential showers. I worked with the builder to construct the concrete-block retaining walls, and the rest of the team set out the other garden features ready for a filming session with the designers and Joe Swift. This was an important day for me as it focused on the building side of things, so I needed my bricklayer there to show this work in progress.

Feeling slightly nervous, I arrived early to brief the students and, most importantly, make sure my builder was ready with concrete blocks and a mortar mix. After an hour or so everyone was ready to do the wall building bit to camera – everyone except my bricklayer. I was mortified (or maybe that should be mortarfied!). Happily it turned out all they needed to see was someone (me) slapping a bit of mortar about and dropping a block vaguely in position while chatting to Joe. But whilst we pulled off that particular deception, no amount of clever angles and astute editing could hide the fact that I was pretty hacked-off and my annoyance was made to look all the worse by Joe Swift's usual calm and relaxed manner.

I watched the show again the other day to refresh my memory and found it no less painful than the first time. My spirits were further tested when I watched the designers explain with great aplomb how *they* had overcome the problem of the electricity cable by reducing the depth of the sunken area and turned this to advantage by creating informal seating at the higher level. They were quoting me pretty much verbatim and it really ticked me off, but spitting out my dummy would have achieved nothing. We still had a job to do – and the rain was continuing to make it as difficult as possible.

By the time of the next shoot, we had all the basic construction works in place but the continuous rain had left every inch of the garden covered in a thick coating of grey-brown mud. It looked pretty terrible, but I was aware of the hard work that lay beneath even if it wasn't particularly photogenic. We stood back as the designers did their bit to camera, and I didn't envy them their attempts to make sense of the devastation that surrounded them.

Bad as that day was, we managed to start the planting. Some trees had been shipped up from the south a day or so earlier and seeing them go into the ground was a pivotal moment for me. The rain poured down as Joe and I struggled in front of camera to plant a large shrub. Joe shouted philosophically (or was it sarcastically?) across to the designers, 'At least we won't have to water it in.'

Despite all the gloom and doom, a glimmer of light suddenly appeared at the end of the tunnel, even if it continued to elude the overcast sky. There was still a long way to go, however, and I knew that the next task might still upset the apple cart.

To achieve the Moroccan styling the clients desired, the design team had decided to finish some of the sunken section with terracotta tiles. These were not just any old terracotta tiles but hand-made, Moroccan mud tiles. I've had many so called frost-proof flower pots fall to pieces at the very mention of the word sub-zero, so I was dubious about this idea. My opinion didn't change when they were delivered. They were pretty rough and many of them had faults and impurities that would compromise their durability. They were great for the floor of your en suite in Marrakesh, but rubbish for anything north of Marseilles.

To protect them against the rigours of the Yorkshire permafrost, they had to be coated twice with some potion that arrived with them. I was given to understand that the milky-white liquid was seriously expensive and almost impossible to find, but I'm fairly sure it was PVA. Hand painting hundreds of tiles was a distraction we could have well done without and led to some friction. I recall one particular moment, about half way through the paintathon, when the BBC's young assistant (or 'gopher' as they are often called) was reduced to tears following an argument with the client. This was a real problem for me because consoling women is way out of my comfort zone, especially at work. It isn't that I'm unsympathetic, I'm just useless at finding the right words.

We managed to coat all the Moroccan mud pies in time for the tiler to do his thing and, after three weeks of toil, mud and tears, we eventually arrived at the final shoot.

175

Our instructions were to leave a few jobs unfinished so they could be completed during filming. Happily, on the day north Leeds was bathed in warm summer sunshine. The students made themselves useful tidying up, the tiler put the last few pieces of dried mud into place, I finished installing the fountain and the designer ladies completed the planting.

On film, Joe says, '*They drew up a planting plan, but I don't think they are sticking to it ... designers' licence.*' If they had a planting plan, I certainly never saw it! Then it was time to make myself scarce and let the TV crew complete their work.

As I left the final scene was being filmed, the one where designer(s), client(s) and presenter are seen chatting and sipping Champagne, and which is usually overdubbed with the credits. I watched for a moment from behind the camera then, after a word with the team, made my departure. I was relieved that it was over and totally exhausted by the physical and mental demands it had placed upon me. Yes, it was a tremendous experience but the end product didn't give me any great pleasure. It was executed well enough and delivered on time, but the concept never really won me over. It was a personal thing, I guess.

The show eventually went out in September, but that wasn't quite the end of the story for me. Several months later, the producer phoned asking me if I would return to the garden to assess a problem. The tiles were already showing signs of degradation and the client, not surprisingly, wanted them fixing. You can take mud out of Morocco, but you can't take Morocco out of the mud!

30

A FEW MORE MINUTES OF FAME

LATER that same year I was asked to look at a property in Ripon with a view to redesigning the front garden. It seemed a routine enquiry at the time; I could never for one moment have imagined where it was going to take me.

I was sitting with my clients in the spacious kitchen of their beautiful Victorian house talking over a few ideas when they mentioned that Charles Dodgson, aka Lewis Carroll, had connections with the property and used to visit a family there. It seemed that his father, the Reverend Charles Dodgson, was Canon of Ripon Cathedral at that time.

As we talked, an idea started to form; what if we approached the BBC for the next *Small Town Gardens* series? I knew they liked the programme to have an interesting angle of some kind – a Moroccan garden in Leeds, for example! – so this seemed perfect. But how would my clients react? Having your garden redesigned is one thing, but having it broadcast to several million TV viewers is another. Whilst this is unlikely to result in thousands of people invading your privacy, it's bound to attract a level of local interest and I could understand them being a little cautious. We talked it through and they went for the idea.

Next day I contacted the series producer who also liked it, but Auntie Beeb was not committed to the idea of a third series so we had to put everything on hold until a decision was made. Happily, it proved to be quite a short wait: the BBC decided to go with series three and we were in.

This alone was good news, but when I learned that one of my fellow contributors was to be none other than John Brookes, I realised I'd be working in very illustrious company. He is the person who had pretty much defined garden design throughout my working lifetime. This was premier-league stuff, and clearly not the time to make a complete balls-up!

I'd already sketched some ideas and the BBC sent up a film crew to interview me working at the drawing board. I was determined to do better than my last performance in front of a camera with Joe Swift back in Leeds, where I resembled a bewildered plank of wood. I needed to appear relaxed and more animated. A bottle of red wine before we started would perhaps, do the trick...

You can't really hide from who you are, and there's no point trying to be Sir Laurence Olivier if you're more of a David Beckham. I decided against the wine but still felt I'd done a bit better, though it was a seriously scary business.

I'd taken the painting of the roses scene from *Alice in Wonderland* as the theme for my design. The scene finds Alice in the garden of the venomous Queen of Hearts, where she stumbles upon the gardeners (otherwise identified as the Two, Five and Seven of Spades) painting roses. The passage reads:

'Would you tell me, please,' said Alice, 'why are you painting those roses?' *- Five and Seven said nothing, but looked at Two. Two began in a low voice, 'Why, the fact is, you see, Miss, this here ought to have been a red rose tree, and we put a white one in by mistake, and if the Queen finds out we should all have our heads cut off you know'.*

It all makes Roald Dahl seem a bit tame, doesn't it?

The main challenge in design terms was to create something that made subtle references to the narrative but was also sympathetic to this fine Victorian home. That meant conveying the essence of the scene without creating some kind of horrendous mini-theme park. Get that wrong and some local hack would no doubt have a field day, with headlines like 'Alice in Blunderland' or 'Mad Hatter Garden Fiasco'.

To stay focused, I avoided any preconceived notions of sculptural gimmickry and concentrated on creating an appropriate rendition of Victorian horticulture. I decided to divide the sloping garden into three square terraces, each trimmed with dwarf box hedges. Into these I would put bedding plants (geraniums): white in one, pink the next and finally red. At the centre of each would be a rose scrambling over an obelisk: white, then red and white multi, then red, indicative of the painting in the story. I'd add some topiary to give a hint of the surreal and hard landscape features that related to the period architecture of the house.

To emphasise the 'wonderland', I brought in a talented artist/ blacksmith to design and fabricate the obelisks and other sculptural pieces to subtly underscore the literary connection. Finally, we would make an application to the local council to remove the front hedge and reinstate the Victorian railings.

The filming schedule was similar to that of the Leeds programme but, as designer rather than project manager, I wouldn't be required on site so much. However, I would be involved in a number of off-site shoots to show how I'd arrived at my final design. The producer asked me to select two locations that had inspired or informed the process so I could visit them and explain their influence. This was part of a theme for the new series where designers would be made more accountable for their proposals, something I wholeheartedly agreed with. It would give the programme a bit of edge, which I believe was the intention.

The BBC invited me down to Ripon to run through schedules with the producer and meet the new presenter, James Alexander-Sinclair. It was clear from the off that James' style was very different to Joe Swift's. In the world of literature, if you think of Joe Swift as Bill Bryson then James would be Shakespeare or Lord Byron. This filled me with dread; if the good old bloke-next-door approach of Joe Swift made me look like a plank, this more theatrical chap would probably marbleise me.

Filming started with an informal chat in the garden. James asked the clients what they would like to see before turning to me for my assessment of the space and an indication of how I would approach the design. I was fine with this, but then they threw me a banana skin. As I prepared to make the presentation, the producer emerged with a laptop loaded with my plan to which I was to refer when making the reveal.

I wasn't in any way precious about my paper drawing, and I can appreciate the advantages of technology when presenting to a large gathering, but referring to a tiny screen and then turning to engage with your audience of three is much more difficult. I would have been happier with everyone standing around the plan so I could point to specific features whilst talking and making eye contact.

I felt more than a little unsettled and sensed the first signs of embalming fluid trickling into my veins. The camera turned to show the garden into which the flamboyant Mr A-S made his entrance by leaping through the sitting-room window. It then showed me, looking rather dumbfounded, trying to convey information to him from the computer from inside the room. He, for reasons best known to himself, attempted to translate what I was describing into some sort of a crazy dance routine and semaphore. It was totally bizarre and I was left looking bewildered and mummified. As I went home, I prayed that the editor might make something of it with a little creative cutting. He didn't.

The plus side of being the designer in these circumstances is that you can, to a great extent, leave the scene of the crime behind you the moment each film shoot is complete – or 'in the can' as we film stars like to say. It was a far cry from my project management episode back in Leeds, where I was constantly getting wet and muddy on site and fire-fighting a range of problems, from disgruntled clients to bolshie, ready-mix truck drivers and tearful BBC personnel. It was a privilege I was quite happy to exercise not long into the build. In pulling out a tatty hedge, it became apparent that the ground level of our garden was slightly higher than that of the neighbours and was held in place by an old brick and stone retaining wall. Having removed the hedge, the wall was now a pile of rubble.

I watched as the project manager did a bit to camera where he said (and I commend his calm delivery): '...*that's causing me a little bit of concern, but nothing we can't see to.*' Meanwhile, I hurriedly got into my car and made my escape.

A few days later I went to Levens Hall in Cumbria for the first of two visits to explain how I'd found inspiration for the design. Levens is one of my favourite gardens, noted for its use of colourful bedding and the most outrageous (and frequently massive) topiary. It is its own kind of wonderland, so I needed to say little to justify myself.

We began with James and I entering the garden via a traditional iron gateway. James asked me what I want from the garden; my reply was measured and articulate, delivered with authority and confidence. As I started to congratulate myself, I heard a voice: '*That was great, John, but can we go again? The sound man picked up some background noise.*'

I listened and heard nothing. We started again; now feeling tense, I tried to replicate my smooth response but instead spewed out some garbled claptrap with all the eloquence of an answer phone.

'*That's fine,*' shouted the director. The crew was off before I could voice my concern and we moved on to scene two.

James asked about the topiary I wanted to use in Ripon, then we sat down to discuss the possibilities. At that moment, he spotted a bus load of Belgian tourists who'd just entered the garden and finished his sentence with a witty reference to their unexpected appearance. I smiled inanely, not having a clue what he's talking about. I sensed my career as a TV presenter swiftly ebbing away.

Our final piece was filmed in an area of tall beech hedges, including a circle about twenty metres in diameter accessed by four evenly spaced gaps. I was to stand in one of the gaps then the camera would pan round to James standing in the next one. Meanwhile, at a given signal, I would run as fast as I could around the back of the camera to the next gap.

On cue, I raced around and hit my mark. I had a split second to assume a nonchalant pose and pull in my middle-aged belly. The camera, that seemed to be turning so rapidly as I was running, now seemed to take ages to pan past me. Once out of shot, I bent forward, grasped my knees and wheezed like an asthmatic sloth.

Just before we finished, the director had an idea for one last sequence. James would walk past one of the gaps, pause for a moment to look in and then continue out of shot. I would do the same from the opposite direction. Surely even I couldn't cock that up?

James strolled into view looking debonair and sophisticated. He turned and glanced quizzically before continuing slowly. I entered from the opposite direction like a dalek, looked to the left with an expression like a rabbit in headlights and made my robotic exit.

Hell, even my walk wasn't photogenic!

On my next visit to Ripon, I discovered that progress was falling behind schedule because of repairing the small retaining wall. Over the next few days I gave what time I could before my next shoot, which was at David Austin Roses down near Wolverhampton.

Being a bit of a rose lover, this was something I'd been looking forward to, but when I arrived I was pretty exhausted, more mentally than physically. After a quick briefing, I was introduced to a lovely lady called Diana, who was being filmed with me in the display gardens. We discussed the roses I might use and I put in my trademark wooden performance, now further impaired by tiredness and anxiety, but Diana was brilliant. She was a natural and I was totally upstaged. I drove home feeling pretty desolate – and very tired.

The day of the final shoot was very close. The hard landscaping was complete and the old privet hedge that lined the front boundary had been replaced with a smart set of traditional railings, but there was still a lot to do. There were about eighty pre-clipped box plants waiting to trim the terraces and half that number of laurel bushes to plant to form new garden hedges.

I sensed that the situation was becoming desperate, so on a bright Sunday morning I drove down with my wife and daughter who had volunteered to help. We beavered away all day until we had planted all the box hedges and given them a final haircut. At about five o'clock the job was done and it looked stunning. I was greatly relieved, but I knew the final shoot would be a frantic affair – and I wasn't wrong.

Throughout the morning I helped with the rest of the planting, breaking off periodically so James could question me about aspects of the garden and I could explain my design philosophy. It seemed to go quite well and I was suddenly aware that the project was finally coming together. Like a jigsaw puzzle nearing completion, the final pieces fell quickly into position. I was taken by surprise when a plaque commemorating the Lewis Carroll connection was screwed onto the brick gate post. It was done, and I just had the final shoot to survive.

After a quick clean-up, James and I were filmed entering the garden chatting about the construction process before perching on a planter for a more detailed discussion. Then my work was done and James went 'centre stage' to give a general summing up. He spoke of the historical context, the literary connection and finished, to my surprise, with a huge compliment: '*I think it is a very fine garden, it works beautifully.*' I was speechless.

The programme went out on Friday 28th of November and I felt rather apprehensive about watching it. As it turned out, I was pleasantly surprised because they had somehow created a pretty decent show. Despite my self-consciousness in front of the cameras, the interaction between James and me had taken on a sort of Holmes and Watson feel, with the flamboyant, eccentric and eloquent Holmes and the practical, plodding Watson. The difference in our manner was emphasised by the fact that he knew exactly what questions he was going to ask, whereas my responses were unrehearsed. In terms of character we were clearly polar opposites, but I really took to the guy. Beneath the theatrical exterior lurked an astute mind and a thoroughly decent bloke.

The day after its broadcast, *The Guardian* devoted ten column inches under the header *Coming up roses*. Gareth McLean wrote:

It was for Carroll that the garden's designer, the arboreally named John Elm, planted the roses, each on a terrace graduating from white through rippled to red. It was his horticultural homage to the painting of the roses in Wonderland. This is not, you will agree, the sort of thing you get on Ground Force...

The story didn't end there. A year later the garden was selected for a British Association of Landscape Industries (BALI) award and I went down to London to be presented with a plaque by Chris Beardshaw. It was a fitting end to what had been two extraordinary years.

31

FLOODS

MY TV moments behind me, I quickly reverted to type and resumed the mantle of landscape rather than garden designer. There were a few garden commissions, including one in Cornwall, but there was no significant change in career. Indeed, the Ripon project was just about my last flirtation with garden design. I had always enjoyed the challenge this presented but concede it was of little real significance and usually benefited just one end user. The concept of a domestic garden is rather a Western one, part of the fabric that makes up our ubiquitous suburban lifestyle. For other people around the world, the notion of such trappings is alien, especially in those climes where people live more at one with their environment.

On Boxing Day 2004, a massive earthquake occurred off the Sumatran coast. The ensuing tsunami affected fourteen countries and took 230,000 lives. It was a truly horrifying event. I watched the news and saw the wreckage of people's homes and belongings strewn across a vast and totally devastated landscape. Events like this invite you to reconsider your personal circumstances and the value of your work. Making a living from designing someone's little patch of suburban Britain suddenly seemed profoundly futile.

Though shocking, destruction of the landscape can be quantified; it is the suffering and despair of the families broken by such an immense force of nature that is so difficult to comprehend. However, in June

2005 I became more than just a distant observer. Following a prolonged period of drought, the heavens opened over North Yorkshire. For several hours the rain poured down at a rate I'd never seen before and the hard-baked soil couldn't absorb it. With the run-off, the usually benign beck that ran beside our garden quickly turned into a torrent. Suddenly our home was under threat.

I watched anxiously as the water level rose to the top of the steep banks and breached the top. Within no time it spread across our garden towards the house. It was a profoundly disturbing experience that made me feel completely helpless. All we could do was anticipate the worst and haul as many items as possible to a position of relative safety.

We watched as the wooden floor tiles detached themselves one by one before floating up on a sea of dirty brown water. Fortunately this ebbed away almost as quickly as it had arrived but it deposited a film of mud, spiced up by the contents of the septic tank forty feet from the back door.

This was not Sumatra. We still had a roof over our heads, unlike those poor souls left traumatised and homeless on the other side of the world. As we dealt with the aftermath of our minor mishap we were reminded of our comparative good fortune as Hurricane Katrina blew in across the Gulf States of the USA. The levées were breached and about half of New Orleans was swamped, with the loss of 1,800 lives and damage estimated to be around US$120 billion.

In no time at all our home was repaired and normality returned, but I feared that would not happen so quickly for the people of west-coast Sumatra and New Orleans. In many respects, it is an abdication of duty on the part of our news media that they never follow up on such tragedies. I believe that seeing, and being invested in, the restructuring of these communities might help us understand and empathise more with people around the world.

Sumatra was an appalling human tragedy, the result of the earth's volatility and something mankind was powerless to do anything about, but can the same be said of Hurricane Katrina? Was this a totally natural disaster, or was the intensity of the storm linked to man's exploitation of the planet?

32

FROM HERE TO AUSTERITY

IN June 2007, Tony Blair resigned as Prime Minister and abandoned his silk-knickered, ermine-trimmed version of socialism to pursue more lucrative opportunities, notably the expansion of his property portfolio. It seemed that socialism had come a very long way since being cradled in the arms of exploited and impoverished manual labourers. Blair handed over the baton to his Chancellor, Gordon Brown. The man who couldn't stop smiling was replaced by the man who didn't know how to – and very soon he had good reason not to.

A year earlier the US bank had raised interest rates, causing thousands to default on their mortgages. This sparked a financial crisis within the US banking system, tremors from which were very quickly felt in the UK. Northern Rock, one of our long-established high-street building societies, had been pursuing a similar model and found itself in financial difficulty. Their plight was merely the tip of the iceberg; suddenly the UK economy was in pieces, together with the economies of pretty much the entire western world.

The banks, those bastions of respectability, had added to their portfolio of indulgences by selling dodgy insurance. Worse still, they were now making investments through the provision of mortgages that they couldn't possibly cover. In the autumn of 2008, Lehman Brothers Bank of New York went bust.

Two months later, Barack Obama was elected US president. He

immediately started formulating a series of policies to stimulate the US economy, notably in connection with what became known as the American Recovery and Reinvestment Act 2009, which, essentially utilised Keynesian theory. The concept is that during times of recession and low private spending, government should increase public spending in order to save jobs and prevent further economic decline by investing in infrastructure, education, health, and now in renewables.

In the UK, the Labour government under Gordon Brown, followed by the Conservative/Liberal government headed by David Cameron, elected to prop up the banks with squillions of quid from the treasury that belonged to you and me. But such benevolence was not so forthcoming for the people like you and me who had been shafted by their indiscretions. With the economy slowing dramatically, many found they could not service their mortgages and many more, including myself, lost their livelihoods.

Further austerity measures were imposed through a raft of cuts to public and social services, notably slashing revenue support grants to local councils. Salaries of local government officers were frozen and councils were forced to cut back on services, reducing the police force by some 20,000 and imposing punitive cuts to welfare, including a bedroom tax on those living in social housing and receiving benefits. Given all this, it is difficult not to take David Cameron's comment, '*What you call austerity is what I might call efficiency,*' as anything other than cynical posturing. He also reneged on his commitment to the environment by slashing incentives to those investing in renewable energy, despite claiming to be sympathetic to green issues.

All this occurred in the wake of the MPs' expenses' scandal, where many of their number made claims for goods and services including hedge trimming (£296), horse manure (£380) and a floating duck island (£1,645). One MP claimed £47 for two copies of a DVD of his own speech – and that was none other than George Osborne, soon to become Chancellor of the Exchequer. The speech was about value for money!

Tony Blair had also been caught with his trousers down, claiming £6,990 for roof repairs to his constituency home in Sedgefield just days before quitting as Prime Minister and resigning as an MP. I can only assume he was looking to reinforce his house in the event of the Iraqis launching their non-existent weapons of mass destruction!

The contrast between the US and UK in response to what was the most serious economic crisis for eighty years is stark. Obama turned the US economy around in little more than two years, whereas we in the UK continued to pursue the policies of austerity for some time. Furthermore, the banks have been bailed out repeatedly with public finance, much of which will never be refunded to the treasury; they have also largely been returned to shareholders to once again pursue their quest for profit at the expense of service and the best interests of the general public.

So how do we make sure this doesn't happen again? You could put a brick through the window of your nearest bank but I don't want to get you into trouble! And, following all the closures, your nearest branch is probably about five miles away so really not worth the effort. In all honesty, I haven't a clue what to suggest but what I would say is this: as long as banks are self-regulatory and unchallenged by outside policing, I see no way it *can* be avoided.

I think the only action left to us is to take a long hard look at our political system and the way we elect our politicians. I would suggest that it is unacceptable to have the country led by a political party that has been elected by little more than a third of the total votes cast in an election, and where only two-thirds of the electorate exercised their right to vote (as in Cameron's last victory).

I believe that democracy is about corporate responsibility, not something left to others. Apathy is no longer an option because it panders to those with vested interests and allows them too much opportunity for deception. Our democracy is sacrosanct and must be protected from those who seek to pervert it for their own purposes.

In its last paper edition, the Independent's front page was dominated by a photograph of the sun setting over the Houses of Parliament with the caption: *A contempt for democracy.* It substantiated its allegation as follows:

- *MPs denied chance to vote on controversial new laws as Government invokes arcane parliamentary loophole to bypass Commons.*
- *Abolition of student grants, fracking in National Parks and contentious new voter registration rules all forced through without proper approval.*

I believe it is incumbent on us all to make those who legislate on our behalf more accountable and transparent in their decision making. We need less politics and more government. There is no point in tutting and accepting the status quo if we feel it is undemocratic and harmful. 'My Voice', a song written by little known (but exceptionally gifted) singer/songwriter Thea Gilmore, pretty much says it all. I will continue to have my voice heard via the ballot box, as I'm sure she will.

33

SWANSONG

SADLY, my marriage came to an end at this time. If this has happened to you, you may know how I felt. It is something of which I am truly ashamed, and it caused so much pain and heartache for people who were, and always will be, near and dear to me.

I'd always believed that this sort of thing didn't happen to people like me, but it seems life is not the gentle stroll in the park I had imagined. Shit, as they say, happens to all of us. I have no excuses.

If all this were not difficult enough, I was also trying to sustain my business during the recession. The financial crash affected many people in many ways; for me it was the impact on housing companies. They stopped building, and with Bellway Homes as my largest client at the time the prospects looked very gloomy.

Desperate times require desperate measures and I had to consider all my options. I couldn't possibly go on under my own steam.

I might not have enjoyed a particularly illustrious career, but I've been very fortunate. I've faced redundancy on several occasions, only to be saved at the eleventh hour. This time was no exception. I'd been mulling over my prospects for a few weeks when a landscape job became available at Middlesbrough Council. I knew the team there, so felt I was in with a chance – and my prospects improved considerably when I discovered I was the only applicant. Such are the difficulties of recruitment in an area of the country continually bad-mouthed by

191

almost the entire nation.

On the 1st of November 2008, I returned to the role of local government officer. I had mixed feelings about the prospect: it was a financial lifeline, but I also had an over-riding sense of failure. I could no longer sustain myself through my hard-won skills, which was a bitter pill to swallow. However, I quickly realised that local government had changed dramatically during the intervening twenty years.

The process of local government seems to have been hijacked by a breed notionally referred to as Human Resource (HR) officers. They sit in grey offices, their desks empty of anything that might look like work, occasionally venturing out to preach their views on political correctness, and diminishing morale with nonsensical team building exercises and dispiriting job evaluations.

In pursuance of their ideology, it now seems to be normal practice to despatch new recruits to be indoctrinated by way of induction courses. I was one such recruit. In fairness, I can't remember much about the course so this is something of an approximation, but I think it gives a flavour of the experience.

I found myself in a room with about a dozen others, being addressed by some kind of multi-purpose, all-inclusive holistic type. We were grouped into teams and given a large sheet of blank paper, then asked to express, with the aid of a box of miscellaneous objects, how we were going to benefit the population. We had a rubber duck, a selection of felt pens, a cheese grater, some Lego, a child's xylophone and a plastic tree. There was a moment of puzzled dismay, then we got down to business.

Someone spewed out a load of cobblers about the cheese grater: the cheese was our team and the action of grating was the staff peeling off to do the work of the Council. I tried to conceal my dismay, but the expression on my face probably betrayed me. Then, to my horror, the fresh-faced college graduate sitting next to me picked up the half-arsed analogy and tried to expand upon it. I noticed our mentor grinning like a Cheshire cat as he tried to tease yet more gobbledegook

192

from his captive audience.

I tried to replace my expression of disbelief with one of enthusiasm and turned my attention to the rubber duck, hoping for divine inspiration. It didn't arrive; what I thought would be a very long day suddenly became a whole lot longer.

Just before leaving some six hours later, we received the results of the Myers Briggs questionnaire we'd completed before embarking on our day of torment. This is a methodology devised to determine your character and identify measures you should consider for self-improvement. Your character type is defined by a series of letters, which in my case turned out to be INTJ, meaning I was an enigmatic, intuitive introvert, who is difficult to know and finds intimacy challenging. I kind of knew that already.

All this understanding yourself, and team building based on role play and anecdotal nonsense is definitely not for me. Would Sir Christopher Wren, Capability Brown and Isambard Kingdom Brunel have benefited from a bit of 'blue sky thinking' before 'running their ideas up a flagpole', only to have them 'kicked into the long grass' by some oik with a diploma in clipboard management? No, they wouldn't – and *they* didn't do too badly. In any case, the basis of landscape design is understanding the complexity of a given environment and interacting with the people within it, often while working with a team of fellow professionals.

Having been inducted to within an inch of my life, I was eventually allowed to start work for Middlesbrough. First I worked on an initiative called the Healthy Towns Project, a government initiative that focussed on diet and physical fitness and was aimed at arresting the rise in obesity. The prize, a share in thirty million pounds, would be awarded to nine towns and cities that came up with the most innovative ideas. Middlesbrough Council's idea of promoting physical fitness and healthy eating through a town-wide programme of urban farming had found favour.

One of my first tasks was to work on the Victorian walled garden at Stewart Park, where I was reacquainted with the legacy of Henry

Bolckow, whose statue I had relocated from Albert Park to the town centre. The walled garden, or what remained of it together with ancillary buildings, potting shed and bothy, were remnants of Bolckow's Victorian estate that went into decline following his death in 1878. It had eventually been sold to the Council in 1924 and the buildings demolished in 1960. In recent times the Council had used the garden partly as a menagerie and partly as a tree nursery.

I had to engage a contractor to clear the site and install a framework of paving. It would then be handed over to a team of young offenders to build a poly tunnel and series of timber planters, and after that to a group of young people with learning difficulties who would start the horticultural aspects. The challenge also required the reinstatement of a crumbling brick archway and removal of an asbestos-roofed shed, all of which needed to be implemented whilst a team of archaeologists excavated the site of the old glasshouses.

It was a fascinating project. On several occasions when I found myself alone there, I could sense the history of the place: moustachioed, bowler-hatted gardeners in humid glasshouses pampering pineapples, cucumbers, orchids and all manner of horticultural exotics while others tended fruit trees and rows of vegetables and salads bound for the dining table at the hall. It evoked memories of Skellow Grange and Uncle Mac tending the gardens for the Humble family.

A tour of the attached bothy, where these hard-working men lived, quickly put all that nostalgia into perspective. Unlike Uncle Mac's cosy estate cottage, this accommodation was bleak and warmed by the smallest fireplaces I've ever seen. It must have been a very hard existence – long days, back-breaking work and precious little in the way of home comforts. Suddenly, being a landscape architect at the beginning of the twenty-first century seemed to be a pretty cushy number!

Work went on at Stewart Park throughout 2009 and we completed the build within the strict time frame; the budget residue was spent on trees and plants to be planted by the first intake of students.

I worked on a number of other major projects. Though not initially part of my remit, I was drafted in to help with the design of several play areas; if I'm honest, these are not something I enjoy doing but they were part of the job. Of more interest, and certainly more challenging, was the redesign of North Ormesby market place, a rather drab and windswept space, on which the Council's engineering department had a million pounds to spend, and Prissick Park where the same department had another £600,000 (courtesy of British Cycling) for the construction of a one-kilometre cycle track.

The cooperation of the market traders was essential to the design at North Ormesby. They were rather truculent, with a spokesman who saw change, no matter how positive, as a manifestation of hell and damnation. As I said earlier, the job of a landscape architect often requires a lot of tact, perseverance and diplomacy.

This was the second major urban space I'd designed in Middlesbrough and with such tasks comes a lot of responsibility. You are designing something the local community will relate to for some time to come, so it's important to get it right. After countless hours of consultation, concept layouts and revisions, we eventually agreed a scheme combining car parking and dedicated market spaces together with – and despite some protests – two lines of trees. Why do people have a problem with trees? They encourage wildlife, add a softness to our hard-edged urban spaces and help purify the air we breathe. So, why do they sometimes cause resentment?

I was also under pressure to agree a suitable site and circuit for the new track at Prissick Park with British Cycling. I had always intended to integrate it into the landscape rather than have it located randomly in open park land; that would have been an easier option, but visually more intrusive in an attractive piece of mature landscape. I had to bite the bullet when I proposed a route that meant felling some existing trees, albeit not particularly mature or good ones. Finally the layout was approved and the race was on to complete the felling programme before the bird-nesting season.

I visited the park a number of times during this period and had second thoughts about what I'd done, but I shouldn't have doubted my decision. Once the track base was down, it all made sense. It sat perfectly within the landscape, much of its length occupying an area defined by mature trees then sweeping through into a young plantation.

It had never been part of my career plan to re-enter the bureaucracy-filled corridors of local government, but I found the work challenging and rewarding. I was now sixty and content to knuckle down and accept that my time at Middlesbrough was a passport to retirement.

Just how wrong can you be?

34

TREASURES, TRIBUTES AND OBITS

IN the summer of 2009, Michael Jackson died. Like so many others at the forefront of show business, his premature death appeared to be mysterious and the loss to the music world was massive. He'd been on the scene for a long time and I think it is something of a tragedy that his much-documented eccentricities and seriously flawed character placed such a stain over his genius. There can be no doubting his ability to perform and he built a whole new genre of music and dance through his talent.

This is probably a good place to make my final comments about the music that, like an artery, has run through my life. It would be impossible to list all the musicians who enriched our lives during what was an amazing period, and I'm saddened by how many we lost prematurely – Buddy Holly, Elvis Presley, Roy Orbison, Dusty Springfield, John Lennon, George Harrison, Jimi Hendrix, Sandy Denny, Gerry Rafferty, Lowell George, David Bowie, Kirsty MacColl, and George Michael, to name but a few.

Happily, there are still a few evergreens to entertain us. As I write, Eric Clapton and Elton John continue to do their thing, as does sixty percent of The Rolling Stones, twenty-five percent of 10cc, and (at the last count) about thirty percent of ELO. I have had the good fortune to see many bands and individuals, some of whom have become national treasures.

Given their massive impact upon a generation, it is not surprising that a new phenomenon arose from the ashes of that dynasty: the tribute band. Groups of anonymous musicians have fashioned themselves into lookalike bands, and some are pretty damned good. From Abba to Led Zeppelin, you can now see virtual copies of just about all your favourite bands. Good luck to them!

In terms of popular music today, there appears to be a belief amongst many producers that money can be made from even the least-gifted performers provided there is an accompanying video featuring half-naked, gyrating females. Even the most talentless of ne'er-do-wells can be elevated to celebrity status through soap opera, reality TV and social media. Much of the contemporary music scene doesn't reach out to audiences in the same way it did when I was young. This is borne out by sales statistics, which show a huge decline in the number of units sold as downloads, CDs or vinyl records. Almost certainly the PC, and the gadgetry that has followed in its wake, delivers home entertainments that has significantly diminished the music industry over the years.

Happily there's been an alternative to all this banality, the roots of which are in the eighties' and nineties' Indie bands, and more recently those covered by the generic term of Alternative Rock. Chaperoning my teenage daughter to the 2002 Glastonbury Festival, I was well entertained by the Dandy Warhols, White Stripes, Doves, Ash, Stereophonics and Coldplay.

It probably says something about the changing times that I was happy to leave the festival early, thereby missing Roger Waters and Rod Stewart. Or maybe I didn't want to be in a five-mile traffic jam trying to escape the car park and was in desperate need of some civilised plumbing, my colon having slammed shut the first time I ventured into the public facilities!

Since then, things seem to have become more difficult for musicians. There is a great wealth of talent out there struggling to be heard through a wall of mundane muzak. I fear for this new breed: the wind of fortune is not behind them as it was for their predecessors whose voices were heard and then promoted by supportive radio presenters. Instead they struggle for air time in a broadcasting media that is a slave to mass appeal. Additionally, the demise of the high-street music store means they have few sales outlets; CDs are now sold by supermarkets, which can hardly be expected to be supportive of new, cutting-edge musicians.

Having been neglected by the mainstream music media, it is up to us to seek them out through such facilities as YouTube. It is so much more difficult than it was in – and yes, I'm going to say it – the good old days!

35

MESSING WITH THE MOTHERSHIP

JUST over a century ago, a North American Cree Indian named Eyes of Fire made an astonishing prophecy. Loosely translated it reads:

One day, because of white man's greed, there would come a time when all the earth being ravaged and polluted, the forests being destroyed, the birds fallen from the air, the waters would be blackened, the fish being poisoned in the streams and the trees would no longer be, mankind as we would know it would all but cease to exist. There would come a time when the 'Keepers of the legend, stories, culture, rituals and myths, and all Ancient Tribal Customs' would be needed to restore us to health, making the earth green again. They would be mankind's key to survival, they were the 'Warriors of the Rainbow'. The 'Warriors of the Rainbow' would spread these messages and teach all peoples of the Earth. They would tell them of how the world today has turned away from the Great Spirit and that is why our earth is 'Sick'.

The 'Warriors of the Rainbow' would show the peoples that this 'Ancient Being' (The Great Spirit), is full of love and understanding, and teach them how to make the earth beautiful again. These Warriors would give the people principles, or rules to follow, to make their path light with the world. These principles would be those of the Ancient Tribes. The Warriors of the Rainbow would teach the people of the ancient practices of Unity, Love and Understanding. They would teach Harmony among people in all four corners of the Earth...'

In other words, it doesn't seem to matter how much we screw things up, salvation is at hand. But a hundred years ago, what might she have envisaged as the worst possible environmental disaster?

Since 1900 the world population has increased by 400 per cent, placing intense demands on our planet. These have been exacerbated by an over-indulgent western society with a seemingly insatiable and unsustainable thirst for energy and material wealth. So, dare we assume that the Rainbow Warriors are prepared for global warming, nuclear waste, genetically modified crops and oceans strewn with plastic? Personally, I would be ashamed to ask.

On the 20th of April 2010, their benevolence would have been tested to the limit when the Deepwater Horizon oil rig in the Gulf of Mexico exploded, spilling an estimated 3.19 million barrels of oil and killing eleven crew. It was the worst oil spill ever in US waters and impacted on a thousand miles of coastline from Texas to Florida. The ensuing damage to the environment (that has been discernible), and more especially marine and coastal habitats, has been massive, and there will be collateral damage for some time to come.

This was just one in a litany of environmental catastrophes that the oil industry has inflicted on the planet during my life time. The *Torrey Canyon* (1967), *Amoco Cadiz* (1978), Ixtoc 1 (1979), *Exxon Valdez* (1989), Kuwait oil fields/Gulf War spillage (1991) and Deepwater Horizon (2010) are etched into our memories. There have been many more, some of which go on insidiously. The Niger Delta, for example, has been abused by various oil companies since 1976 with a spillage estimated at something like 2.4 million barrels and still increasing to this day.

All these accidents and disasters cause possibly irreparable damage, contaminating sources of drinking water and polluting the land and our oceans. Whilst we may point an accusatory finger of guilt at the oil companies, we must all accept responsibility for the damage we are inflicting on the planet, whether by oil spills or by burning fossil fuels in pursuit of our excesses.

Here in the UK it is now some fifty years since our discovery of the

North Sea oil field, which we were told would expedite the nation's economic recovery. We sat back and cheered our good fortune, oblivious to the consequences; the term 'global warming' had not yet reared its ugly head. This should have been the time for our government to start formulating an energy policy that looked beyond this finite resource to more sustainable options, but instead it opted for short-termism, blindly cashing in on the windfall with no thought to the future.

Only a few years after the discovery E. F. Schumacher in his seminal book *Small Is Beautiful* addressed this. He made the case for natural resources to be viewed as capital rather than income, stating:

A businessman would not consider a firm to have solved its problems of production and to have achieved viability if he saw that it was rapidly consuming its capital. How, then, could we overlook this vital fact when it comes to that very big firm, the economy of Spaceship Earth and, in particular, the economies of its rich passengers.

He continues:

...we have indeed laboured to make some of the capital which today helps us to produce – a large fund of scientific, technological, and other knowledge; an elaborate physical infrastructure; innumerable types of sophisticated capital equipment, etc, – but all this is but a small part of the total capital we are using. Far larger is the capital provided by nature, and not by man - and we do not even recognise it as such. This larger part is now being used up at an alarming rate, and that is why it is an absurd and suicidal error to believe, and act on the belief, that the problem of production has been solved.......First of all, and most obviously, there are the fossil fuels. No one, I am sure, will deny that we are treating them as income items although they are undeniably capital items. If we treated them as capital items we should be concerned with conservation; we should do everything in our power to try and minimise their current rate of use; we might be saying, for instance, that the money obtained from realisation of these assets – these irreplaceable assets – must be placed into a special fund to be devoted exclusively to the evolution of production methods and patterns of living which do not depend on fossil fuels at all or depend on them only to a very slight degree.

That Schumacher wrote this in 1973, long before global warming was even thought about, makes it all the more remarkable. Regrettably the subsequent lack of investment and vision, notably in the field of renewable energies, now leaves us facing an energy crisis. Many of our politicians, together with their predecessors, have ignored the problem, preferring to focus their attention on unsustainable economic expansion. Even in the nineties, when terms like 'global warming' and 'hole in the ozone layer' became common parlance, we continued denying their existence.

When the problem was officially recognised, notably within the Kyoto Agreement of 1997, many leading nations still failed to legislate comprehensively. The American Congress did not ratify its recommendations and President Bush rejected it entirely in 2001. What we really needed was a no frills, impartial presentation of the facts.

Salvation, or at least hope, came in 2006 by way of a film entitled *An Inconvenient Truth*, presented by Al Gore, who had been narrowly and controversially defeated (or not?) by Bush in the presidential election of 2000. In presenting this film, I suspect Al Gore probably did more as a defeated candidate than he ever might have achieved in office. If you haven't seen the film I urge you to do so. There are still deniers, usually those with significant interests in the oil business, but there is now a general acceptance of the fact that carbon-based energy is greatly impacting on the earth's climate and eco systems.

The extraction and burning of fossil fuel to supply our insatiable thirst for energy is only part of the problem now challenging our environment and wellbeing. In the early fifties, nuclear energy was starting to be seen as the silver bullet that would solve our energy requirements. Our post-war government commissioned research into nuclear power, resulting in the opening of Calder Hall Power Station (later Sellafield) in 1956. The Queen opened the plant stating:

'This new power, which has proved itself to be such a terrifying weapon of destruction is harnessed for the first time for the common good of our community.'

Oppenheimer's weapon of mass destruction that brought a swift end to WW2 by eradicating the Japanese cities of Nagasaki and Hiroshima and some 130,000 lives was now to become our best friend, boiling our kettles, warming our baths and bringing heat and light into our homes. Unfortunately within a year the monster's old habits resurfaced when a fire broke out in the neighbouring Windscale plant causing a release of radioactive contamination that registered a five on the international nuclear-event scale where the worst-case scenario is a seven.

The potential for nuclear disaster has raised its head several times since then. In 1979, at Three Mile Island, Harrisburg, Pennsylvania, an event rated a five, and at Chernobyl, Ukraine, an explosion and the ensuing fallout warranted a seven. Both incidents were the result of human error. Mother Nature has also proved that she can undo our best-laid plans. At Fukushima in 2011, the nuclear reactor was catastrophically damaged by a tsunami following the Tohoku earthquake, effectively disabling all the safety measures. The result was another grade seven incident.

Even if it were possible to build a fool-proof, indestructible nuclear power station, how do we safely dispose of the nuclear waste? That has never been resolved. Here again E. F. Schumacher had cautionary words:

No degree of prosperity could justify the accumulation of large amounts of highly toxic substances which nobody knows how to make 'safe' and which remain an incalculable danger to the whole of creation for historical or even geological ages. To do such a thing is transgression against life itself, a transgression infinitely more serious than any crime ever perpetrated by man. The idea that a civilisation could sustain itself on the basis of such a transgression is an ethical, spiritual and metaphysical monstrosity. It means conducting the economic affairs of man as if people really did not matter at all.

Three years later, in 1976, a report by the Royal Commission on Environmental Pollution, concluded:

...It would be morally wrong to commit future generations to the consequences of fission power on a massive scale unless it has been

demonstrated beyond reasonable doubt that at least one method exists for the safe isolation of these wastes for the indefinite future.

Whether or not Eyes of Fire could have foreseen the threat to the planet posed by nuclear fission is difficult to tell, though I think it unlikely. And I'd be very surprised if she had any inkling of the possibility that the boffins of the twenty-first century would be messing about with genetically modified organisms (GMOs). But here we are. The boys and girls in white coats have created a moral dilemma to test us: genetically modified food crops.

The large companies responsible for their development produce compelling arguments to justify their genetic gerrymandering, feeding off statements such as the one made back in 1997 by the United Nations proclaiming that eighteen million people die annually in less-developed countries from hunger and under-nourishment. It makes a very persuasive argument, but is it the whole story? Are these huge corporations truly altruistic in their ambition?

I've done some research to better understand the pros and cons but have found much of the scientific information in the public domain unhelpful. It is very much a case of we say X, they say Y. Nevertheless, I am sceptical of the claims put forward by companies like Monsanto, not least because their record on openness about health and the environment leaves much to be desired.

My first concern is the assertion that GMOs are needed because the world is unable to sustain and feed its population. At the moment this is a rather simplistic hypothesis as it disregards the impact of world politics, greed and waste. Remember Bob Geldof's words in 1985? '*It was pathetically obvious that in a world of surplus, starvation is the most senseless death of all.*' Some thirty years on he is probably wondering why nothing has changed despite his efforts and those of many other people, not to mention a whole plethora of world-aid organisations. If anything the problem is worse today.

But, I hear you say, since when has Geldof been an authority on world population and the production and distribution of food? I suspect he knows a lot more than most, but that's irrelevant as his statement is substantiated by many august bodies and learned people who advance the same argument backed up by telling statistical evidence. Did you know that the so-called advanced nations waste at least thirty percent of the food they have at their disposal?

That is only half of the problem. Dietary preferences within these nations are hopelessly unsustainable. Consider the amount of land needed to produce red-meat products in relation to its potential output for cereal crops, or the amount of water it takes to produce one bottle of Australian wine. Quite simply, we cannot go on consuming like this forever. I'm not saying you have to give up your rump steak and Shiraz completely, but intake of these foods has to be moderated. If we are serious about feeding the world, a completely new dietary regime will be required for all of us.

Sadly, current attitudes in the West give little cause for optimism. What message are we sending out to the world when we talk about obesity becoming a national problem while other sections of the same community need to use food banks? If we choose not to be sympathetic to the less fortunate members of our own society, what hope is there for street kids begging in any one of a dozen African nations?

This is only one aspect of the debate. We also need to examine how GMOs might impact on our environment and whether they deliver all that is expected of them. It is claimed that genetic modification can produce crops that are drought resistant, weed resistant and can be stored for longer than traditionally produced foods; however, the companies promoting their use have no means of knowing how they might impact on the wider environment. What might happen if GM plants become dominant at the expense of diversity, thereby damaging our ecology? In the long term, how might they impact on DNA within the food chain?

My research suggests that GM crops are being sold under strict control of the manufacturers, thereby tying farmers into restrictive covenants that prevent them from using other products. It has also been said that they are engineered so as not to produce a seed crop. If that is the case, farmers who might want to save a third of their harvest for the next year's sowing can't do so and will have to buy new seed. It seems that these big corporations might not be the philanthropists they would have us believe and there is a hidden agenda in play.

Henry Kissinger, former US Secretary of State, once said, '*Who controls the food supply controls the people.*' Alarming as that may be, the greed of western society (or those subscribing to it) is contributing to the suffering of other nations around the world. As Mahatma Gandhi famously said, '*Earth provides enough to satisfy every man's needs, but not every man's greed.*'

My lifetime has seen us move along the road to potential environmental oblivion. Denial and prevarication by our political leaders, and their historical failure to confront these issues, means the word 'crisis' is common political parlance – energy crisis, environmental crisis, food crisis etc. – suggesting that they, and their predecessors, had nothing to do with it.

In the USA, the oil lobby remains unstoppable. When speaking of Shell and BP, Jonathon Porritt, said:

'*The senior managers of these companies know, as an irrefutable fact, that their current business model threatens both the stability of the global economy and the longer term prospects of mankind as a whole*'.

Given this sad history of denial, it beggars belief that even now we are disregarding the evidence and statistics that warn us of impending environmental disaster. Back in 2008, when receiving the Democrat Party nomination for the presidency, Barack Obama stated, '*this was the moment when the rise of the oceans began to slow and our planet began to heal*'. They were brave words from someone seeking election where a huge proportion of the nation's economy is based on burning carbon fuels.

This prompts me to address the question I posed in an earlier chapter. Could the intensity of Hurricane Katrina have been exacerbated by climate change? As I write, the consensus of scientific opinion suggests that it is difficult to make a judgement because, whilst there is a wealth of historical records for levels of rainfall and temperature, there is little information about the intensity and number of hurricanes. Nevertheless, it is generally accepted that the rise in sea level, something conclusively attributed to climate change, places sea defences at greater risk from storm surges and increases the rainfall associated with such events. It is clear that the ingredients were in place for this disaster, as is the potential for generating similar disasters in the future.

I was excited by Obama's victory and had high hopes that he might lead the USA in new directions, not least in its policies for the environment and climate change. The President of the USA is, after all, generally regarded as the most powerful man in the world. Initially the omens looked promising; he was successful in stimulating the sagging economy by establishing the American Recovery and Reinvestment Act in which he demonstrated a commitment to clean energy, created 225,000 'green' jobs and provided incentives to save energy both in industry and homes. He also encouraged the motor industry to increase the fuel efficiency of its new products, all of which indicated a strong determination to reduce greenhouse gases. Sadly, he managed rather less than we hoped. His Clean Power Plan, aimed at capping carbon emissions and slowing oil production, was thwarted by a Republican senate, the Republicans traditionally being supported by the oil business.

Our response to the energy crisis in the UK concerns me greatly. It has been glacially slow in evolving and our governments, notably that of David Cameron, were quick to abandon initiatives and electoral promises on economic grounds. Yes, we have invested in macro schemes, such as wind farms and some solar farms, but the solution to our energy shortfall requires a broader approach that encompasses more diverse thinking and opportunities.

I am astonished that construction companies, notably house builders, have for so long been allowed to continue building homes with little attention to energy conservation other than double glazing and rudimentary levels of insulation. Their reluctance to install features such as solar panels, triple glazing and more sophisticated methods of heat retention are based on the premise that such technology renders the product too costly for the buyer. If that is the case, the government needs to provide financial incentives to see that these features are installed on all new builds. However, I am not entirely convinced by the builders' claims, not least because the CEO of one company recently paid himself a bonus of £110m, suggesting that green issues are an unwelcome distraction.

Rather than actively exploring these alternatives, UK governments have preferred to place emphasis on the technologies I described previously. They have built a new phase of nuclear power stations, even though the technology is capable of catastrophic environmental disaster and waste products present insurmountable disposal problems. Similarly, they have endorsed fracking for oil-shale gas, which perpetuates the burning of fossil fuels, something we know is changing our climate and which has the potential to deliver serious harm on a local level by polluting fresh-water aquifers, destroying wildlife habitats and causing long-term damage to local economies.

It is very disturbing to contemplate this process being actioned not in some God-forsaken wasteland of North Dakota but in the green fields of North Yorkshire amidst villages and small towns. If that wasn't reason enough not to proceed with fracking, the fact that it is of dubious economic worth should be – but there are interests at stake that may not necessarily be to the national good and the wellbeing of the environment.

Our government has adopted a stance on GMOs whereby the planting of genetically modified crops is not permitted unless it is backed by a risk assessment; that's rather like saying you can't produce nuclear energy unless you can guarantee the waste can be safely disposed of. Internationally, I fear the genie is now well and truly out of the bottle. Powerful corporations within the USA are using their influence to foist GM products upon us, even when their impact on the environment is an unknown quantity.

By our over-indulgence, we have allowed some to view the environment as a smörgåsbord of money-making opportunities. We are blindly pursuing the politics of greed with little care for environmental consequences with none of our world leaders appearing eager to take on the mantle of Rainbow Warrior.

We seem to have little appetite for curbing our excesses even though we know this will deliver massive food shortages, environmental devastation and life-threatening climate change. It raises a very frightening prospect expressively depicted by David Attenborough, when he said: '*How could I look my grandchildren in the eye and say I knew what was happening to the world and did nothing?*'

Kirsty McColl cleverly voices my fears with a song titled 'Maybe It's Imaginary', from her 1991 *Electric Landlady* album. Please seek it out.

I've said my piece, and you will have detected more than a hint of despondency and exasperation, but I have not given up altogether on human nature. My admiration for the Native Americans has been further enhanced and I appreciate the faith and belief emanating from the words of the Cree Indian, Eyes of Fire. Whatever your beliefs, it is a remarkable gesture of benevolence toward a world which has, in many respects, shown nothing but antipathy toward the entire native population of North America.

36

ANNUS HORRIBILIS

I'M not normally given to cursing and swearing, but I feel justified in describing the twelve months that followed as outstandingly f*****g terrible. In my heart I knew there were challenges ahead – my marriage was finished and my mother's health was in decline – but I had no inkling of all that was to follow.

As the year wore on, my mother became increasingly frail. She had suffered a mild stroke and was now dependant on carers and regular visits by family and friends. Driving home one evening after one such visit I experienced a severe headache, which came as quite a shock. Convinced that I was also having a stroke, I went straight into A&E at The Friarage Hospital, Northallerton to be checked out.

For about an hour I sat waiting, during which time someone stuck a skewer into my left temple every few minutes – at least, that's how it felt because the pain was excruciating. It was so bad that a nurse took me to one side and gave me a few painkillers before a doctor, examined me. These were the industrial strength, 'I can't feel my legs' painkillers. I hadn't felt that way since misguidedly attempting a fourth pint of Newcastle Brown back in the Leeds Union some forty years previously.

A little later I was led to a cubicle. A young female doctor appeared and, after some biro chewing, book thumbing and Googling, determined I was afflicted with trigeminal neuralgia. The trigeminal nerve down the left side of my face had decided to make my life a misery. There wasn't a lot they could do, other than blasting me with steroids, giving me some pills and telling me to take a few days off work.

A couple of days later I staggered upstairs to the bathroom where everything went black. Moments later, I discovered I was prostrate in the bath. Fortunately the noise of my fourteen-stone frame collapsing into the tub didn't go unnoticed. As I regained consciousness, I could hear concerned voices calling my name and someone banging on the door.

As I extricated myself and staggered into the bedroom, it occurred to me that this was starting to look a little serious. That suspicion was confirmed when two burly paramedics appeared at the foot of the bed. They decided I had developed a urinary tract infection (UTI) and, taking into consideration my other ailment, offered me the choice of a ride to A&E plus a three-hour wait to see a doctor (it was Friday night) or staying home and waiting for an out-of-hours doctor to call round.

I opted for the home visit. It was well into the small hours when he arrived, but he was quick to reassure me. I needed to get my urine back to a shade of straw yellow rather than Americano coffee, and for that I needed to see my GP for a prescription.

I quickly became worse. My pee did become more yellow – but so did my face. My energy levels plummeted and I felt breathless. However, I persevered. I saw my GP a couple of times over the next few weeks without making progress, constantly telling myself that he knew best. He didn't.

Following a series of tests, it was noticed that my kidneys were producing results, that went beyond 'cause for concern' and bordered on 'why isn't he dead?'. I was immediately taken off the pills, which I later discovered were in a dosage that could clear up a UTI in a herd of elephants. There were more tests and, to my horror, I was told I had chemically-induced hepatitis brought on by the toxic cocktail of medication. A few months earlier I had been a reasonably healthy sixty year old; now I was a wheezing wreck struggling to tie my shoelaces without gasping for breath.

Weeks passed during which time I made slow progress. Then came the call I'd been dreading, even if it wasn't entirely unexpected: my mother had passed away. Several weeks earlier she had been admitted to the local cottage hospital because of her steady decline. During that period, my visits revealed a person who had done her job in life and was now seeking her own peace.

I joined my brother at the hospital for our final goodbyes and found her laid out in her room with the bright summer sunshine pouring in through the window. Her face looked calm and serene, as though twenty years had fallen away from her. She had fulfilled her family duties and nursed my father when he was losing his battle with Parkinson's disease until his death ten years earlier. She was now released from worldly existence with all its trials, and I took great comfort from seeing the transformation. It was the right time for her – and I certainly would not have wanted her to witness the problems heading in my direction.

I returned to work towards the end of June but found little appetite for the job. Morale at the Council was generally low because of the severe and, in my opinion punitive, cuts being levied by central government. When the opportunity arose to take voluntary redundancy, I didn't take much persuading.

My plan was to catch up with some former clients and hopefully secure a steady flow of commissions to keep me going for a few more years, but not long after Christmas that plan was in tatters.

For some time I had been aware of another health problem; I was passing copious amounts of blood when I went to the toilet. Choosing to ignore this and the bowel cancer test kit I'd received several months earlier were not the best decisions I've ever made. Finally I returned to the doctor, who immediately referred me to hospital.

If you have ever had to deal with health problems of a similar nature, you will probably share my hatred of words that end in -oscopy. For those of you who haven't, that means shoving a camera up or down any bodily orifice to gain access to your various tubes and important bits. It's not like they're using a 35mm Pentax fitted with a telephoto lens, it just feels like it!

Having survived the ordeal and then spent an hour or so recuperating on a bed, I expected to be given a box of pills and sent on my way. Instead, I was ushered into a tiny room for a chat with the consultant and a senior nurse. I was now a little worried and with just cause; the series of photographs I was shown identified a cancerous tumour in my lower bowel. I was stunned and hardly dared to look at the pictures. The consultant's words went unheeded; my senses were numb.

I can't really recall how I felt when the news eventually sank in; I suspect it was along the lines of 'is this actually happening to me?'. I had no contingency plan for this scenario; it isn't really something you plan for.

Then there was all the difficult and emotional stuff. How would I break the news to friends and family? What would happen to my work? Would I actually survive? I was suddenly pitched into some kind of alternative reality, totally detached from all that had gone on in my life.

There were tears, but I was not bitter or driven to ask the question why me. There is no answer to that, no matter how many times you ask it. We all know not only how commonplace the disease is, but also how indiscriminate.

I first understood this when the athlete Lillian Board died of cancer back in 1970, at the age of just twenty-two and barely two years after winning a silver medal at the Mexico Olympic Games. In more recent times it had shown itself twice to me, on both occasions claiming the lives of former work colleagues.

It seemed these sobering occurrences, together with the number-crunching of informed authorities, had subconsciously primed me for such circumstances. It didn't diminish the initial shock to my system – I don't believe anything can – but when the dust had settled, I was more level headed about it than I'd thought possible. Or, more likely,

I hadn't really absorbed the scale of the threat.

In the wake of the initial colonoscopy, my terrible twelve months concluded with a flurry of medical treatment and procedures. A CT scan on the 13th of February, and sigmoidoscopy (little brother of colonoscopy) on the 21st, both at The Friarage Hospital, Northallerton, were followed by five sessions of radiotherapy at James Cook Hospital in Middlesbrough. It was the NHS at its very best, working with speed and efficiency, for which I remain exceedingly grateful.

As I recall, no prognosis was ever offered nor did I ask for one. It was all very matter of fact. The consultant surgeon was going to remove the offending chunk from my bowel and then perform an ileostomy, where the small intestine would be diverted through an opening in my stomach through which I would pass waste material. Having no control over my bowel movements and having to wear a bag was a prospect I found very difficult to come to terms with even though the process might be reversed.

I was admitted to hospital on the 30th of April, a very grey day in every respect. I said my goodbyes before being ushered into a bland room where a hospital gown was laid out ready for me. Having nervously done battle with its fastening ties I sat deep in thought, those thoughts becoming ever deeper and more reflective, confused and disorientated.

Moments later, I was loaded onto a trolley and taken to the operating theatre where my ordeal would begin.

37

MEMO FROM A HOSPITAL BED

I returned to consciousness as I was wheeled through doors into a ward. It was dark. I was aware of people walking beside me but was far too drugged up to understand what they were saying. Everything seemed to be surrounded by a bright, psychedelic chequerboard of constantly moving imagery that was tunnelling my vision. It was all pretty weird and soon became more so.

My trolley driver did a well-rehearsed three-point turn and reversed me neatly into my position in the hospital's Intensive Therapy Unit, or ITU. Apparently the operation hadn't been all plain sailing and the surgeons thought it prudent to monitor me closely for a while before I went onto a general ward.

I remember there was a bit of a huddle around my bed while one of the nurses explained to me that the button control in my right hand would allow me to self-administer pain killer. The system is regulated so you don't massively overdose, which I certainly would have done – my right thumb was popping away like a teenager sending a text message. The downside of this, as I quickly found out, was that it completely screwed up my mind when it came to sleeping. The first night was particularly terrible; I had constantly changing, kaleidoscopic hallucinations. I was totally away with the fairies.

I was pretty much comatose for a couple of days. The limited daylight from the narrow windows and the low-level lighting rolled day into night. Nurses constantly buzzed around checking my blood pressure and temperature, occasionally replacing the IV drip bags, while the one who had pulled the short straw periodically emptied my stoma bag. They went about their duties with good humour and efficiency, doing what they could to lift my spirits, but I was totally out of it. I had to stop pressing the junky button because it was frying my brain. My morphine-fuelled psychedelic flights of fancy came to an abrupt halt when in came the physiotherapist and cold turkey.

Naively I had thought that it was simply a case of undergoing an operation then being pampered back to health before being discharged back into the world. What I hadn't factored in were the antics of the sadistic physiotherapist. On day three I was suddenly and unceremoniously dragged from my dream world by a young fellow called Nigel, who was either the spawn of my officious secondary-school PE teacher or a product of the Hitler Youth. His positive demeanour and bulging biceps gave a clear indication of his intention: to give me acute pain and discomfort. Egged on by a gallery of baying nurses, I was extricated from the safety of my warm bed and invited to take a turn about the ward.

If I'm honest, both he and the nurses were very supportive; they needed to be because my first attempt at standing up was brief and would have ended in a nose dive had they not been in attendance. Undaunted, Nigel eased me up again for further punishment. I took a tentative step forward carrying the catheter bag in my right hand while a nurse hoisted the drip that was feeding into the back of my left hand.

I completed two lengths of the ward before heading back towards my welcoming bed, but I was redirected into the bedside chair where I crashed like a bag of spuds. My pelvic area quickly became extremely painful and my head slumped into my chest. I managed to sit like that for a few minutes before being helped back onto my mattress, where I receded into melancholy.

Next day Nigel put me through my paces again and I did a little better, though the pain in my bum was still excruciating. Day three of my physiotherapy was brightened by the arrival of Holly, one of Nigel's colleagues. She helped me do about eight lengths of the ward at a canter before easing me back into the torture chair. What the hell was wrong with my backside? The reason soon revealed itself to me in all its shocking, multi-coloured glory.

A day or so later, one of the nurses asked me if I'd like a bacon sandwich. I'd hardly eaten anything up until then. That seemingly trivial thing marked a turning point in my recovery. Someone had sensed my despair and comforted me with a smile and a culinary kiss. Having softened me up with a bacon butty, I was then invited to take a shower.

'How's that going to happen with all these tubes sticking out of me?' I asked.

'Oh, that's easy,' came the confident reply. 'I'll help you into a special wheelchair, and wheel you, plus drip stand, into a wet room. I take your gown off and shower you down. Simple.'

A few minutes later, I was sitting naked in the shower with the warm water splashing over me. Until then I'd not felt inclined to look at the carnage that had befallen me but I could now survey the damage not hidden by the white bandage protecting the area of the incision. From my belly button down and, as far as I can deduce, all around my pelvic area, I had every shade of bruise imaginable. So that was why my arse was killing me.

Sunday the 6th of May started bright and sunny. I was deemed fit enough to be transferred onto a ward where I started counting ceiling panels, as you do when your brain is completely numb. It was, however, the calm before the storm.

By mid-afternoon I was feeling distressed and I called for assistance, but the nursing team had been drawn away to a problem elsewhere. It was only at the beginning of the afternoon visiting period that my difficulties were investigated.

My recollections of the next forty-eight hours are sketchy. I recall being taken for a hastily organised CT scan and a conversation with my consultant, but I can't remember what he said. After that, it was a total blank.

I was in a bad way. An internal bleed was flooding my pelvis, and my consultant and his team were quickly back into action. I was unconscious for the next twenty-four hours; when I eventually returned to the land of the living, I was back in ITU surrounded by a vast array of equipment and tubes. I felt both poorly and frightened. The fantastic nursing staff in ITU did what they could to lift my spirits but we all knew the road back from here would be long and arduous.

It wasn't until the physiotherapy started again that I improved, but even then I was seriously incapacitated. I'd been in hospital for more than two weeks, a week longer than the original estimate, and was now confronting mental demons in addition to my physical discomfort.

I eventually made it back to the surgical ward, and that's when a new series of roller-coaster highs and lows started. Adjusting to the ward was difficult. To start with, the ratio of nurses to patients was less favourable; in ITU it was pretty much one to one, but here you were required to be a bit more self-aware and less dependent. Days and nights seemed never ending; I grew weaker through not eating sufficiently and was alarmed by the huge intake of pills being served up.

It was another low plateau and I was slipping into a pretty despondent mindset. I needed something to buck this worrying direction and the first glimmer of hope came about on the back of a passing comment. It was so inconsequential that I don't suppose the person involved even realised it, but it meant a great deal to me.

It happened following the regular morning rounds of the surgical team. Having considered my condition for several minutes they moved away, but as they did the registrar whispered, '*You're a very strong man, John.*' She will probably never know just how much positivity came from those few words, and I would love to thank her for playing a small but very special part in my eventual recovery. Like the nurse with the bacon sandwich in ITU, her moment of personal caring was much appreciated. It was the act of someone who understood the profession, an act that is the very essence of hospital treatment.

I had several weeks to observe just how hard these people work. It's insane; they have so much to do that it's almost impossible for them to take time out to talk to patients and yet that is so important in aiding recovery. Bless you, every one of you.

I received a further tonic a few days later when my daughter and her long-term partner paid an unexpected visit. It wasn't the way I'd have chosen to be told of their engagement, but it was the best medicine ever. Now I had to get better!

As they left, a strange mixture of joy and sadness washed over me: great joy in seeing my daughter so happy and very much in love with a really special young man, but at the same time sadness at my failings in life and the realisation that I was being superseded without any means of redemption.

Just over a week later I was sitting in bed watching the ward TV, anticipating a lunch of poached salmon, new potatoes and peas followed by strawberries and fresh cream. How do I remember this? It was the day of the Queen's Diamond Jubilee and the hospital catering team had pulled out all the stops, which is a sight more than can be said for the so-called Thames Jubilee Pageant that unfolded in front of Her Majesty. It was yet another London fiasco, reminiscent of the disastrous 'River of Fire' millennium fireworks flop.

Who the hell thought this up? A ride on the Thames followed by having to stand in appalling weather conditions while more than six hundred boats slowly dribbled by? Was that the best we could do to show our love and appreciation for someone who has dedicated their life in service of their country for sixty years?

Suddenly, and rather unexpectedly, there was talk of me being discharged. All I had to do was prove I could walk a little way and negotiate a flight of steps to the satisfaction of a physiotherapist. With Holly supporting me on one side and a nurse on the other, I was ready to sprint the length of Northallerton High Street! It was a while since I'd negotiated a staircase and I had no idea how I'd manage, but I did. Then it was out into the sun-drenched car park.

As we passed through the entrance door, my senses were

220

overwhelmed by the summer heat and the sweet smell of newly-cut grass. It was the best medicine I could have had and I made light of my task. It was official: next morning I could leave.

I drifted off to sleep that evening thinking of packing my clothes and going home, but there was one final twist to my confinement: I woke with a temperature. Not only that, there was talk of my kidneys not being one hundred percent. The bad news was broken to me that I wouldn't be going home. Worse still, I needed further investigation by a urologist which meant being transferred to James Cook Hospital in Middlesbrough.

I was devastated. I turned to the nurse sitting at my side and wept. Loved ones came to see me in the afternoon but I was like a man condemned. As they left, a paramedic eased me into a wheelchair then into a waiting ambulance. I looked out of the window and watched the rain falling from a slate-grey sky, washing away all my optimism of the previous afternoon.

James Cook Hospital was claustrophobic and very different to what I'd become accustomed to at the Friarage. My bed was between two others in a cramped ward of six. It was after eleven at night when a very tired urologist finally came to see me having been detained in an operating theatre. He was apologetic but he needn't have been; I could see how exhausted he was. Happily he had good news: I seemed to have stabilised and he was content to monitor my progress without further intervention.

I hardly slept for the next two nights before being returned to the Friarage. I stayed there one more night, then was finally discharged on the 12th of June. I had received the finest medical attention the NHS could offer, and for that I shall always be very grateful.

38

CARRY ON REGARDLESS

I'D made it through the greatest ordeal of my life and now began the task of reinventing myself. I knew I would never be the same person again and the road back to any semblance of my former self would be a long and difficult one. Helen Rollason, the BBC's first female sports presenter, had a very clear understanding of this when, in a moving and inspirational account of her own battle with cancer, she wrote:

I'm just an ordinary person learning to live as best I can with a body that has gone wrong, and with a strong belief that if I get my mind right, it can make quite a difference to my life expectancy.

Helen lost her battle but I understood where she was coming from and hoped I might be blessed with a fraction of her courage.

My regime was along the lines of 'ignorance is bliss'. I preferred the word 'denial' to 'remission', and tried hard not to become a hypochondriac at the slightest sniffle or twinge. My resolve was soon tested.

Life at home got off to a shaky start. I'd been in the hospital for almost seven weeks, during which time I'd never seen myself in anything larger than a small bathroom mirror. When I did, I was horrified; two stone in weight had fallen off me, my face was gaunt, the bulk in my chest and shoulders had migrated to my middle, and my legs had withered away to bean poles. I was never a George Clooney lookalike but I hoped I'd retained a little rugged charm into middle age, so seeing myself had a profound effect on my mental state. Time spent in bed rebuilding my strength gave me opportunity for negativity and self-pity. There were occasions when, for no obvious reason, I burst into tears. To this day, I am given to emotional outbursts at unlikely moments and without any prompting.

Underpinning my recovery was my partner, who was no stranger to cancer. She had supported me steadfastly and now stood by me as I began the challenge of rebuilding my life. We were also helped by frequent visits from community nurses who came to re-dress the wound in my lower belly and change my stoma bag.

Despite everyone's best endeavours, I made slow progress and it was starting to look like I might not make the window of opportunity for chemotherapy. I went back to hospital to be assessed by the oncologist, who promptly discounted the possibility; my nearly passing out in the waiting room probably informed his decision. There was nothing more to do but continue to build myself up by eating, as prescribed by my surgeon, 'all the things you're not supposed to eat'. I slowly increased my weight and strength, whilst at the same time acclimatising to my new plumbing.

As I started to feel better, I thought about restarting my business and quickly picked up a small design project. Without any warning, however, my plans were once again in tatters. About a year after the first diagnosis, I was told that a CT scan had revealed some irregularities in my liver. I was quickly referred to St James's Hospital in Leeds for an MRI scan. The results were revealed a couple of weeks later: it was cancer again.

The prognosis was delivered honestly, brutally even, but this was not the time for procrastination. If I did nothing, I would not last five years; with an operation to resection my liver, I had a 50% chance of doing so.

Little over a week later, I was in a waiting room at St James's Hospital with other poor souls awaiting their operations. It was a bland space, the walls sparsely adorned with uninteresting posters warning of various symptoms and diseases. They encircled a group of people for whom such worries were now of little consequence.

I was eventually called, prepared for the operation then wheeled to theatre – but there was a glitch when the anaesthetist's mobile phone rang. It seemed there wasn't a bed for me. Then her phone rang again; we were back on and a few moments later I was counting my way to unconsciousness.

Following the operation I was taken to a peaceful ward in a new part of the hospital where I felt immediately at ease. I even dared to contemplate an early discharge date, and on the 31st of March, five days after admission, I returned home. My battle now was to be well enough to give my daughter away at her wedding on the 18th of May.

Other than a bit of a scare when the wound turned septic, prompting a brief hospital visit, my second recovery was rapid and I would be able to take advantage of chemo. Another shock awaited me, though, when I was notified of two anomalies on my lungs. I tried to focus on the planned chemo regime and read all the supporting material, but in all honesty I hadn't a clue what to expect when I turned up for the first session.

As I entered the room, patients were sitting quietly reading books as they received their chemo. The atmosphere was calm and the nurses attentive yet low key, ensuring their clients were comfortable and relaxed.

After completing the paperwork, a cannula was inserted into my left hand and the liquid started to flow into my body. As the infusion progressed, my arm began to stiffen and tingle with cold. It was disturbing, but to some extent I was prepared for it as I'd read about this sensitivity to extremes of temperature.

For the next three weeks I took chemo tablets, then had a week off before the cycle started again. The plan was for me to undergo a total of four cycles, and during this period, I accepted the inevitable that my career was over. I was not physically capable of the tasks required of a landscape architect, so I started to wind up the business.

I phoned former clients, my professional institute and accountant, then faced up to parting company with my trusty drawing board that had sustained me for many years. It was a sad day because its removal, more than anything else, symbolised both the end of my professional working life and the end of an era. The boys and girls with the magic boxes and screens had taken over and I bemoaned the loss of human touch in the design process. But that's the way it is now. For a dinosaur like me, it was most definitely the end but I'd had a long career and hopefully one that had brought some small improvements to the world.

There was no time for regrets or looking back; I had a wedding to prepare for. My daughter was getting married and I was determined to give her away in the time-honoured tradition. *My* marriage had ended and I was physically half the man I'd been little more than a year earlier, but on that memorable day I had a feeling of renewal that eclipsed any desire to dwell in the past. As I walked my daughter across the field to the tiny church, there could be no prouder dad in the world.

EPILOGUE

IT'S hard to believe but more than eight years have passed since I sat alone with my thoughts in pre-op at Northallerton Hospital. I was looking into an abyss without any clue about how my life was to change, or my life expectancy. In the weeks that followed there were times I didn't think I would even make it out of hospital. It was the greatest challenge I've ever – and hope will ever – face. A milestone in my recovery came in 2018 when my oncologist discharged me; it was every bit as emotional as the moment I was told I had cancer, perhaps even more so.

I have come to terms with the fact that I'm physically not what I was and I can't do all the stuff I used to enjoy, or at least to the same level. It's not just simply the physicality of these things, it's the mental adjustments you need to get to grips with. I'm aware that some people experience life-changing moments through adversity and I'd dearly like to tell you that being seriously ill was spiritually enlightening, but I can't. There has been no psychological epiphany; I simply blunder along life's road with all the same day-to-day hang-ups, regrets and guilt trips. But these feelings are part of life itself, and I figure if I'm still challenged by such things then I still have a part to play.

But I do believe the intimacy of my confinement in hospital actually made me a better social animal. I try harder to interact with others, the simple, yet supremely important, process of people investing in people. An exchange of pleasantries, a handshake and a hug from a friend or family member means so much more to me. I feel more self-assured and better equipped to deal with small talk, something I could never do as a self-conscious youth.

Whilst there may not have been a road to Damascus moment of enlightenment, my appreciation of life has changed in several ways. I have always gained pleasure from our living environment and this aspect of my life has taken on even greater significance. It's as if someone has polished my glasses and opened up another corner of my brain. More than anything, I feel privileged and grateful to live in a land of beauty and abundance. I love the varied landscapes and diverse cultural history of this country and am saddened when I see them being taken for granted or, worse still, abused and neglected. I also find myself less tolerant of those who want to damage our society wilfully, or because of greed.

I have no time for anything that spawns social injustice and inequality and despise those who justify them as the inevitable consequence of modernity, often with little more than a resigned shrug of the shoulders. I believe we will have to take stock of the many challenges facing the western world if we are to prevent its decline and fragmentation.

I suspect we may also have to be more demanding of our political system and its leaders and more selective of new technologies, pursuing those based on need and wellbeing rather than greed and indolence. Similarly, we will have to temper the unsustainable demands of the shareholder driven economy and adopt a lifestyle that protects our environment and is less corrosive. That's a tall order, but I believe these changes will be forced on us by circumstance if we don't make them voluntarily.

We need to act if those who define our lives are failing us, if not for ourselves then for our children. I know that in the time it took me to pluck up courage to approach a publisher my text has been overtaken by events, few of which give me cause for optimism. We have increased the rate of global warming, stoked the flames of ethnic and religious intolerance around the world, unleashed the horrors of Covid-19 and endured the nightmare of Donald Trump. However, I have not given up altogether. I find hope in the young environmental activist Greta Thunberg who is prepared to take on those who despoil the planet. We have also, to some extent, rediscovered the soul of our nation through the remarkable deeds of centenarian Captain Sir Tom Moore. These two people have almost restored my faith in mankind, so I look to the future with at least a modicum of hope.

$$\odot\odot\odot$$

Well, here we are. My literary scrapbook is complete and the process of cobbling together my thoughts and memories has been a cathartic one. Although challenging at times, it made me reconsider my life, my emotions and my opinions in a way I hadn't done before, and probably never would have done without my encounter with cancer. I'm sure many of you will disagree with some of my opinions and that's fine by me; it is the mark of a free society to do so, and that is something for which, despite all my gripes and grumbles, I am truly grateful.

I know that in many ways I have been fortunate. My generation has been blessed by a cultural revolution that enriched millions of lives, a true renaissance. The evolution of rock music alone has given immeasurable pleasure to millions of people like me. I hope my song references have illustrated how this impacted on my lifetime and rekindled a few memories for you.

As regards my future, who knows? I shall continue to enjoy the time I have and cause as little damage as possible. When the inevitable happens, I intend to depart this world with little ceremony. You may well have detected that I have a rather jaundiced view of religion, largely because of the radicals and extremists who lay claim to it and seek to diminish those who do not share their beliefs. My religious beliefs lay somewhere between the pagan notion of the 'Green Man', a fairly liberal interpretation of basic Christianity and maybe just a dash of Shintoism. Let's just say I'll be happy to depart this world having attempted to live as best I could by the simplest, most basic Christian ways, and I am happy for others to seek solace as best they can when it is their turn. Or, as the wonderful Irish comedian, Dave Allen, put it, '*May your God go with you.*'

With love,

John Elm

My thanks:

To all those I have quoted (including many who are no longer with us) either through their spoken words or their writing. You have entertained, informed, inspired and occasionally troubled me deeply.

Robert Louis Stevenson
Harold MacMillan, The Earl of Stockton
George Bradshaw – *Railway Handbook* (1863)
Sir Bobby Charlton – *My life In Football*
Gary Imlach – *My Father And Other Working Class Football Heroes*
Martin Peters – *The Ghost Of '66*
Kenneth Wolstenholme
Sir Geoff Hurst – '*1966 World Champions*'
Mark Powell – *Notes to reissue of* 'Days Of Future Passed', *The Moody Blues*
Rob Young – 'Electric Eden : Unearthing Britain's Visionary Music'
Neil Armstrong
Jimmy Page
Eric Clapton – self-penned notes to his album *Me and Mr Johnson*
Colin Escott – notes to the BB King album *His Definitive Collection*
Jimi Hendrix
Sir Winston Churchill
John Maynard Keynes, Lord Keynes of Tilton
Baroness Margaret Thatcher
Voltaire
Michael Hanrahan
St Francis of Assisi
Lord Geoffrey Howe
Harry Enfield
Sir Jonathan Porritt
Paul Menzies – *Britain In Photographs: Middlesbrough Past And Present*
Sir Bob Geldof – *Introduction to Live Aid* , compiled by Peter Hillmore
Nelson Mandela

The Independent

Graham Rice – *Evening Standard*

William Wordsworth – extract from *The Excursion*

Donald Rumsfeld

Tatanka Yotanke (Sitting Bull)

Kim Wilde

Stephen Hawking

Sir Billy Connolly

The Rt Hon. David Cameron

Alan Bleasdale – *Boys From The Blackstuff*

Joe Swift

Charles Dodgson aka Lewis Carroll – *Alice's Adventures In Wonderland*

James Alexander-Sinclair

Gareth McLean – *The Guardian*

Tony Blair

Eyes of Fire (North American Cree Indian)

Mahatma Gandhi

E. F. Schumacher – *Small Is Beautiful*

Henry Kissinger

Sir David Attenborough

Barack Obama

Helen Rollason – *Life's Too Short*

Dave Allen

To the many and varied songwriters and musicians whose work has enriched my life and illuminated my script.

'Rock Island Line', Clarence Wilson 1929 – (Lonnie Donegan cover 1955)

Singin' The Blues', Guy Mitchell 1956 – (Tommy Steele cover 1957)

'Gamblin' Man', Woody Guthrie, arr. Lonnie Donegan (Lonnie Donegan 1957)

'Telstar', Joe Meek (recorded by The Tornados) 1962

'Love Me Do', John Lennon & Paul McCartney (The Beatles) 1962

'It's My Party (And I'll Cry If I Want To)', Walter Gold, John Gluck Jr., Herb Weiner & Seymour Gottlieb 1963 (Dave Stewart & Barbara Gaskin cover 1981)

'A Hard Rain's a-Gonna Fall', (from the album *The Free Wheelin' Bob Dylan*), Bob Dylan 1963

'She's Not There', Rod Argent (The Zombies) 1964

'Eve Of Destruction', Barry McGuire 1965

'My Generation', Pete Townshend (The Who) 1965

'Heart Full Of Soul', Graham Gouldman (recorded by The Yardbirds 1965)

'Dead End Street', Ray Davies (The Kinks) 1966

'Sunny Afternoon' Ray Davies (The Kinks) 1966

Revolver (album), The Beatles 1966

Bert And John (album), Bert Jansch and John Renbourn 1966

'2 Days Monday', Mike McGear, Roger McGough, Mike Gorman (The Scaffold) 1966

Sgt Pepper's Lonely Hearts Club Band (album), The Beatles 1967

'San Francisco (Be Sure To Wear Some Flowers In Your Hair)', John Phillips (recorded by Scott McKenzie 1967)

'Feels-Like-I'm-Fixin'-To-Die Rag', Country Joe McDonald 1967

'Say You Don't Mind', Denny Laine 1967 (Colin Blunstone cover 1971)

'All You Need Is Love', John Lennon & Paul McCartney (The Beatles) 1967

'Ob-La-Di, Ob-La-Da' (from *White Album*), John Lennon & Paul McCartney (The Beatles) 1968

What We Did On Our Holidays (album), Fairport Convention 1968

'Give Peace A Chance', John Lennon (Plastic Ono Band) 1969

'Since I've Been Loving You' (from the album *Led Zeppelin III*), John Paul Jones, Jimmy Page & Robert Plant 1970

'Alright Now', Andy Fraser & Paul Rodgers (Free) 1970

'Whitey On The Moon', Gil Scott-Heron 1970

'American Pie', Don McLean 1971

'Stairway To Heaven', (from the album *Led Zeppelin IV*), Jimmy Page

& Robert Plant (Led Zeppelin) 1971

'I Don't Believe In Miracles', Russ Ballard 1972 (recorded by Colin Blunstone)
'Wishing Well', Paul Rodgers & Simon Kirke (Free) 1972
Henry The Human Fly (album), Richard Thompson 1972
Tubular Bells (album), Mike Oldfield 1973
I Want To See The Bright Lights Tonight (album), Richard Thompson. Richard & Linda Thompson 1975
'The Dimming Of The Day' (from the album *Pour Down Like Silver*), Richard Thompson. Richard & Linda Thompson 1975
'Bohemian Rhapsody', Freddie Mercury (Queen) 1975
'Anarchy In The UK', Glen Matlock, Steve Jones, John Lydon & Paul Cook (Sex Pistols) 1976
Rumours (album) – Fleetwood Mac – 1977
Saturday Night Fever (album), various writers/artistes (primarily The Bee Gees) 1977
'Baker Street', Gerry Rafferty 1978
'Wuthering Heights', Kate Bush 1978
'The Man With The Child In His Eyes', Kate Bush 1978
'Sultans Of Swing', Mark Knopfler (Dire Straits) 1978
'Wired For Sound', Alan Turney & BA Robertson 1981 (recorded by Cliff Richard)
'Drive', Ric Ocasek (The Cars) 1984
'Do They Know It's Christmas', Bob Geldof & Midge Ure 1984 (recorded by Band Aid)
'Between The Wars' (EP), Billy Bragg 1984
'Road To Hell', Chris Rea 1989
'Maybe It's Imaginary' (from the album *Electric Landlady*), Kirsty MacColl 1991
'Goodbye England's Rose' ('Candle In The Wind'), Elton John & Bernie Taupin 1997
'Dad's Gonna Kill Me', (from the album *Sweet Warrior*), Richard Thompson 2007

'My Voice', (from the album *Ghosts And Graffiti*), Thea Gilmore (with Billy Bragg) 2010

And last, but by no means least, my love and thanks to all the team at 2QT publishing, especially:
Catherine Cousins, for guiding me through the process, Karen Holmes, for her encouragement and patience in making sense of my ramblings, and Hilary Pitt for the fabulous artwork.

Lightning Source UK Ltd.
Milton Keynes UK
UKHW010928071221
395242UK00006B/843